MW01233953

THE COMPLETE NINJA FOODI 2-BASKET AIR FRYER COOKBOOK FOR BEGINNERS

1200 Days of Delicious Recipes for Complete Meals using DualZone

Technology|Full Color Pictures Version

KAREN A. BURKS

Copyright© 2022 By Karen A. Burks Rights Reserved

This book is copyright protected. It is only for personal use. You cannot amend, distribute, sell, use, quote or paraphrase any part of the content within this book, without the consent of the author or publisher.

Under no circumstances will any blame or legal responsibility be held against the publisher, or author, for any damages, reparation, or monetary loss due to the information contained within this book, either directly or indirectly.

Disclaimer Notice:

Please note the information contained within this document is for educational and entertainment purposes only. All effort has been executed to present accurate, up to date, reliable, complete information. No warranties of any kind are declared or implied. Readers acknowledge that the author is not engaged in the rendering of legal, financial, medical or professional advice. The content within this book has been derived from various sources. Please consult a licensed professional before attempting any techniques outlined in this book.

By reading this document, the reader agrees that under no circumstances is the author responsible for any losses, direct or indirect, that are incurred as a result of the use of the information contained within this document, including, but not limited to, errors, omissions, or inaccuracies.

Table of Contents

Introduction   1

Chapter 1
Basics of Ninja Foodi 2-Basket Air Fryer   2
Understanding your Air Fryer   3
Cleaning and Maintaining your Air Fryer   4
Cleaning and Caring for Ninja Foodi 2-Basket Air Fryer   4
Air Fryer Cooking Tips   5
Ninja Dual Zone Air Fryer Cooking Tips   5
Questions, Notes and Helpful Advice   6
Frequency Asked Questions & Notes   6
Helpful Advice for Ninja dual zone air fryer   7

Chapter 2
Snacks Recipes   8
Hot Avocado Fries   9
Bacon-wrapped Goat Cheese Poppers   9
Crabby Fries   10
Hawaiian Ahi Tuna Bowls   10
Herbed Cheese Brittle   11
Savory Sausage Balls   11
Chili Corn On The Cob   12
Rich Egg-fried Cauliflower Rice   12
Bacon & Blue Cheese Tartlets   13
Spiced Roasted Pepitas   13
Mozzarella En Carrozza with Puttanesca Sauce   14
Cheeseburger Slider Pockets   14
Crispy Okra Fries   15

Artichoke Samosas   15
Cheesy Spinach Dip   16
Parmesan Crackers   16
Onion Puffs   17
Crispy Chicken Bites with Gorgonzola Sauce   17

Chapter 3
Breakfast Recipes   18
Pumpkin Muffins   19
Egg and Avocado in The Ninja Foodi   19
Sweet Potatoes Hash   20
Bacon and Egg Omelet   20
Yellow Potatoes with Eggs   21
Egg with Baby Spinach   21
Banana and Raisins Muffins   22
Bacon and Eggs for Breakfast   22
Sweet Potato Sausage Hash   23
Air Fried Bacon and Eggs   23
Air Fryer Sausage Patties   24
Hash Browns   24
Egg White Muffins   25
Perfect Cinnamon Toast   25
Bagels   26
Banana Muffins   26
Donuts   26

Chapter 4

Poultry Mains Recipes — 27
Fajita Stuffed Chicken — 28
Almond Chicken — 28
Bagel Chicken Strips — 28
Crispy Curry Drumsticks — 29
Chicken Cordon Bleu — 29
Chicken Parmesan — 30
Thyme Duck Breast — 30
Spicy Roasted Chicken — 30
Marinated Chicken Legs — 31
Spicy Chicken Thighs — 31
Crispy Chicken Breasts — 31
Stuffed Chicken Breasts — 31
Gingered Chicken Drumsticks — 32
Glazed Chicken Drumsticks — 32
Sweet Potato-Crusted Chicken Nuggets — 33
Southern Style Chicken — 33
Simple Chicken Thighs — 34
Simple Turkey Breast — 34
Lemon Feta Chicken — 35
Buffalo Chicken — 35
Crispy Chicken Legs — 36
Parmesan Chicken Breasts — 36
Rosemary Turkey Legs — 37
Garlicky Duck Legs — 37

Chapter 5

Beef, Lamb, and Pork Recipes — 38
Exotic Beef and Plum Dish — 39
Beef and Grape Roast — 39
Peas and Beef Mix — 39
Paprika Beef — 39
Oregano and Asparagus Pork — 39
Simple Beef Rib Eye — 40
Beef Schnitzel — 40
Garlic and Bacon Platter — 41
Beef and Tomato Balls — 41
Mango Pork Fillet — 41

Chapter 6

Fish and Seafood Recipes — 42
Honey-Glazed Salmon — 43
Baked Grouper with Tomatoes and Garlic — 43
Fried Catfish Fillets — 43
Steamed Tuna with Lemongrass — 43
Tuna Steak — 43
Sesame-Crusted Tuna Steak — 44
Simple Buttery Cod — 44
Cod with Jalapeño — 44
Scallops in Lemon-Butter Sauce — 44
Bacon-Wrapped Scallops — 44
Fried Prawns — 45
Blackened Fish — 45
Oyster Po'Boy — 45
Trout Amandine with Lemon Butter Sauce — 46
Fried Catfish with Dijon Sauce — 46
New Orleans-Style Crab Cakes — 46
Mediterranean-Style Cod — 47
Fish Sandwich with Tartar Sauce — 47
Lemony Prawns and Courgette — 47
Roasted Fish with Almond-Lemon Crumbs — 47

Chapter 7

Vegetables and Sides Recipes — 48
Chickpea Fritters — 49
Potatoes & Beans — 49
Mushroom Roll-Ups — 49
Bacon Potato Patties — 49
Herb and Lemon Cauliflower — 50
Acorn Squash Slices — 50
Green Tomato Stacks — 50
Healthy Air Fried Veggies — 51
Fried Patty Pan Squash — 51
Air-Fried Radishes — 51
Bacon Wrapped Corn Cob — 51
Breaded Summer Squash — 52
BBQ Corn — 52
Delicious Potatoes & Carrots — 52
Lemon Herb Cauliflower — 52
Broccoli, Squash, & Pepper — 53
Sweet Potatoes & Brussels Sprouts — 53
Rosemary Asparagus & Potatoes — 53
Air Fryer Vegetables — 54
Garlic-Rosemary Brussels Sprouts — 54
Balsamic Vegetables — 55
Flavourful Mexican Cauliflower — 55

Chapter 8

Desserts Recipes — 56
Bread Pudding — 57
Mini Strawberry and Cream Pies — 57
Mini Blueberry Pies — 57
Lemony Sweet Twists — 57
Air Fryer Sweet Twists — 58
Fudge Brownies — 58
Churros — 58
Apple Fritters — 59
Pumpkin Muffins with Cinnamon — 59
Fried Oreos — 59
Grilled Peaches — 60
Strawberry Nutella Hand Pies — 60
Baked Apples — 60
Cinnamon Sugar Dessert Fries — 60
Lava Cake — 61
Jelly Donuts — 61

Appendix 1 Measurement Conversion Chart — 62
Appendix 2 Air Fryer Cooking Chart — 63
Appendix 3 Index — 64

Introduction

Heart problems are one of the biggest threats in today's world. No one dies instantly from heart problems but they suffer over years. The treatment is quite costly so it can also cause financial damage as well. Somehow people are not very aware of it before the big damage. But if you are aware of it, congrats, you are one step ahead of everyone. The main reason for heart problems is gaining extra weight. Being overweight just not causes heart problems but fatal diseases like diabetes, acne, idleness, and many more.

Being overweight has many reasons behind it. This can happen because of family tradition, eating too much sugar, and eating oily food. Oily food is the main reason behind gaining extra weight and a key ingredient to heart problems. The problem is everyone likes fried and oily food. Who would refuse a juicy steak from their plate? And who won't like a crispy and tasty burger in the evening? Oily and fried food is indeed tasty but it is not healthy at all. Consuming oil can increase the cholesterol level and it can cause heart problems like blockage and stroke.

Feeling worried? It is normal to feel sad about leaving your favorite food for your health. What is the meaning of living longer without tasty food right? Well do not worry, I felt the same long ago. One of my loved ones faced a heart problem and he liked fried food over anything. As a fried food lover I realized that the same thing can happen to me. Then I found an alternative to deep-fried and oily food.

I started using Ninja Foodi 2-Basket Air Fryer and after that my life changed a lot. At first, I thought it wouldn't be tasty and that I would give up in a short time. But I was proved wrong because of the taste and facility this air fryer can provide. Air fryer fried food tastes even better and it is healthy. An air fryer requires very little oil and no oil in many cases. Less oil means less cholesterol and a healthy heart with a happy tummy. An air fryer can cut oil usage up to 70% to 80%.

An air fryer is not just healthy but it is also safe for your wallet. An air fryer is like a small oven with much more facilities. The good thing is, this air fryer uses half as much electricity compared to a micro oven. In this case, it is saving you from extra energy bills and future treatment bills as well.

By using an air fryer you are also helping nature as well. An air fryer uses less electricity compared to an oven which means less carbon in the atmosphere. Where an oven takes up big space in your kitchen, and an air fryer can fit into any corner.

Understanding your Air Fryer

The Ninja Foodi 2-Basket Air Fryer has a double chamber facility. You can cook two different items at the same time at different temperatures. Basically, it is a two-in-one air fryer. This model has six different modes for cooking different dishes. The extra crisp mode is for cooking items like chicken nuggets and french fries. On the other side, there is a baking mode for baking cakes, pastries, and anything bakeable. The dehydrating mode is for dehydrating meat, fish, and vegetables. It also has an air fryer mode for frying dishes with less oil. There is a reheat mode that allows you to reheat your food without changing the quality. You are also getting a roast mode that turns the air fryer into a roaster. This device is incredible compared to other devices on the market. There is no competition for The Ninja Foodi 2-Basket Air Fryer.

A big reason for not buying an air fryer is its maintenance. In this case, you are lucky, this specific version is very easy to maintain and clean. You can take out the baskets separately and clean them with soap and water, just do not scrub them harshly. Scrubbing hard might cause damage to the materials. This device is totally rustproof so there is no reason to worry about using soap water.

Some people think air fryers are only made for frying food but it is not true at all. You can cook many things in an air fryer, especially in the Ninja Foodi 2-Basket Air Fryer. It might feel hard to use it for the very first time. But do not worry this machine is very easy to navigate. With this cookbook in your hand, you can cook like a professional chef within a few days.

As I used this air fryer myself, I have written solutions to the problems I faced. It will be a useful cookbook for anyone. You can use it yourself or gift it to your friends and they will be grateful to you. I have mentioned many famous and easy dishes in this book. Not only common recipes but I have enlisted all many unique recipes that you won't find anywhere else. From breakfast to dinner and starter to the main dish everything is in this book. Non-veg, veg, dessert, fries, there is everything in this book.

I tried these recipes myself and I served them to my friends too. All of them left licking their fingers. The temperature control is so easy and effective it will help to cook it how you want. I have mentioned every recipe in detail like time, quantity, color, and everything. You won't face any problem trying out new recipes for the first time.

A person who has never cooked in their entire life can easily cook with the help of this cookbook. As the Ninja Foodi 2-Basket Air Fryer does not come with a default cookbook you can take this cookbook for granted. Everything is explained in detail from how to use and how to clean.

As an author, I have worked very hard on this book. I hope everyone will be helped by my recipes and pray for me. Have a tasty and crispy day!

Cleaning and Caring for Ninja Foodi

2-Basket Air Fryer

Following each use, you must give the device a thorough cleaning. Whenever you want to clean your device, make sure it is unplugged from the wall.

MAIN UNIT

Use a moist cloth to wash the product and the control panel. WARNING: DO NOT SUBMERGE the product in any kind of liquid. Dishwashers should never be used to clean the main unit.

CRISPER PLATES

Both the dishwasher and manual washing are suitable for crisper plates. You may either let everything dry naturally or dry it with a towel if you wash it by hand.

BASKETS

A dishwasher or hand washing is acceptable for these baskets. Dry all components by either letting them air dry or patting them dry with a towel if you're hand washing them. We advise hand washing your basket to ensure its longevity. Put the plates or baskets from the crisper into a sink full of warm, soapy water to loosen any food particles that may be adhered to them.

Ninja Dual Zone Air Fryer Cooking Tips

If you're using the Ninja Air Fryer for the first time, remember to preheat it for 3 minutes at 200°C to eliminate any manufacturing smells.

For frozen foods, preheat the air fryer for 5 minutes at 199°C to ensure that your food cooks evenly.

After the preheating cycle is completed, add your food to the baskets and ensure the food is not touching the sides of the baskets to avoid uneven cooking.

If you wish the cooking in both compartments to finish at the same time (when foods have different temps, times, or cook functions), select the desired cooking function in Zone 1 and Zone 2, press SYNC, and then press the start button to initiate cooking in the zone with the longest cooking time. The other zone will display Hold, and the unit will beep and activate the second zone when both zones have the same time remaining.

If you wish to cook a larger amount of the same food, put ingredients in the baskets and insert them in both zones. Select the desired cooking function, temperature, and time. Press the MATCH button to copy the zone 1 settings to zone 2. Then Press' start' to begin cooking in both zones.

Remove the food using silicone-tipped tongs or utensils.

Questions, Notes and Helpful Advice

Frequency Asked Questions & Notes

How do I change the time or temperature if I only use one zone?
When only one zone is on, the up and down arrows can be used to alter the time or temperature at any time.

How do I change the time or temperature when both zones are in use?
Choose the zone you want, then use the arrows next to TEMP to alter the temperature or the arrows next to TIME to change the time.

How do I take a moment or stop one zone once using both zones?
Choose the zone you want to stop or start playing in, and then press this same START/PAUSE button.

When air-frying, why do some ingredients fly around?
From time to time, the air fryer's fan will move light foods around. Use made of wood toothpicks to keep food like the top bread slice on a sandwich from falling off.

Can I air-fry things that are wet and battered?
Yes, but make sure you use the right breading method. It's essential to coat foods with flour, egg, and bread crumbs in that order. So that crumbs don't get blown away by the fan, press the breading firmly onto the battered items.

What caused a circuit breaker to trip while the unit was being used?
The unit utilizes 1690 watts of electrical power, so it needs to be plugged into a 15-amp outlet. If you plug a plug into a 10-amp breaker, the breaker will trip. When the unit is in use, it is also essential that it is the only thing plugged into an outlet. Make sure the unit is the only thing plugged into an outlet on a 15-amp blocker to avoid tripping a breaker.

Helpful Advice for Ninja dual zone air fryer

Make sure the ingredients are laid out evenly and without overlap on the bottom of the drawer for consistent browning. Make careful to shake the ingredients halfway through the designated cooking time if they are overlapping.

You can alter the cooking temperature and duration at any moment.

Simply choose the zone you wish to change, then use the TEMP or TIME arrows to change the temperature or the time.

Reduce the temperature by 10°C if you're converting recipes from your normal oven.

To prevent overcooking, periodically check your food.

On occasion, the air fryer's fan will fling light meals in all directions.

Secure food with cocktail sticks, such as the top slice of bread on a sandwich, to help with this.

For consistent, crisp results, the crisper plates elevate the ingredients in the drawers so that air can circulate under and around them.

Pressing the dial after choosing a cooking function will start cooking right away. The temperature and time settings on the device will be used.

Use at least 1 tablespoon of oil when cooking fresh veggies and potatoes for the best results. To obtain the required level of crispiness, add extra oil as needed.

For the best outcomes, keep an eye on the food while it cooks and take it out when the required level of brownness has been reached. In order to keep track of the interior temperatures of meat and fish, we advise utilising an instant-read thermometer.

To achieve the greatest results, take food out of the oven as soon as the cooking process is finished.

Chapter 2
Snacks Recipes

Hot Avocado Fries

Cook time: 20 minutes | Serves 2

- 1 egg
- 2 tbsp milk
- Salt and pepper to taste
- 1 cup crushed chili corn chips
- 2 tbsp Parmesan cheese
- 1 avocado, sliced into fries

1. Preheat air fryer at 375°F.
2. In a bowl, beat egg and milk.
3. In another bowl, add crushed chips, Parmesan cheese, salt and pepper.
4. Dip avocado fries into the egg mixture, then dredge into crushed chips mixture to coat.
5. Place avocado fries in the greased frying basket and Air Fry for 5 minutes.
6. Serve immediately.

Bacon-wrapped Goat Cheese Poppers

Cook time: 10 minutes | Serves 10

- 10 large jalapeño peppers
- 8 ounces goat cheese
- 10 slices bacon

1. Preheat the air fryer to 380°F.
2. Slice the jalapeños in half. Carefully remove the veins and seeds of the jalapeños with a spoon.
3. Fill each jalapeño half with 2 teaspoons goat cheese.
4. Cut the bacon in half lengthwise to make long strips. Wrap the jalapeños with bacon, trying to cover the entire length of the jalapeño.
5. Place the bacon-wrapped jalapeños into the air fryer basket. Cook the stuffed jalapeños for 10 minutes or until bacon is crispy.

Crabby Fries

Cook time: 30 minutes | Serves 2

- 2 to 3 large russet potatoes, peeled and cut into ½-inch sticks
- 2 tablespoons vegetable oil
- 2 tablespoons butter
- 2 tablespoons flour
- 1 to 1½ cups milk
- ½ cup grated white Cheddar cheese
- pinch of nutmeg
- ½ teaspoon salt
- freshly ground black pepper
- 1 tablespoon Old Bay® Seasoning

1. Bring a large saucepan of salted water to a boil on the stovetop while you peel and cut the potatoes. Blanch the potatoes in the boiling salted water for 4 minutes while you Preheat the air fryer to 400°F. Strain the potatoes and rinse them with cold water. Dry them well with a clean kitchen towel.
2. Toss the dried potato sticks gently with the oil and place them in the air fryer basket. Air-fry for 25 minutes, shaking the basket a few times while the fries cook to help them brown evenly.
3. While the fries are cooking, melt the butter in a medium saucepan. Whisk in the flour and cook for one minute. Slowly add 1 cup of milk, whisking constantly. Bring the mixture to a simmer and continue to whisk until it thickens. Remove the pan from the heat and stir in the Cheddar cheese. Add a pinch of nutmeg and season with salt and freshly ground black pepper. Transfer the warm cheese sauce to a serving dish. Thin with more milk if you want the sauce a little thinner.
4. As soon as the French fries have finished air-frying transfer them to a large bowl and season them with the Old Bay® Seasoning. Return the fries to the air fryer basket and air-fry for an additional 3 to 5 minutes. Serve immediately with the warm white Cheddar cheese sauce.

Hawaiian Ahi Tuna Bowls

Cook time: 20 minutes | Serves 4

- 8 oz sushi-grade tuna steaks, cubed
- ½ peeled cucumber, diced
- 12 wonton wrappers
- ¾ cup dried beans
- 2 tbsp soy sauce
- 1 tsp toasted sesame oil
- ½ tsp Sriracha sauce
- 1 chili, minced
- 2 oz avocado, cubed
- ¼ cup sliced scallions
- 1 tbsp toasted sesame seeds

1. Make wonton bowls by placing each wonton wrapper in a foil-lined baking cup. Press gently in the middle and against the sides. Use a light coating of cooking spray. Spoon a heaping tbsp of dried beans into the wonton cup.
2. Preheat air fryer to 280°F. Place the cups in a single layer on the frying basket. Bake until brown and crispy, 9-11 minutes. Using tongs, carefully remove the cups and allow them to cool slightly. Remove the beans and place the cups to the side. In a bowl, whisk together the chili, soy sauce, sesame oil, and sriracha. Toss in tuna, cucumber, avocado, and scallions. Place 2 heaping tbsp of the tuna mixture into each wonton cup. Top with sesame seeds and serve immediately.

Herbed Cheese Brittle
Cook time: 5 minutes | Serves 4

- ½ cup shredded Parmesan cheese
- ½ cup shredded white cheddar cheese
- 1 tablespoon fresh chopped rosemary
- 1 teaspoon garlic powder
- 1 large egg white

1. Preheat the air fryer to 400°F.
2. In a large bowl, mix the cheeses, rosemary, and garlic powder. Mix in the egg white. Then pour the batter into a 7-inch pan (or an air-fryer-compatible pan). Place the pan in the air fryer basket and cook for 4 to 5 minutes, or until the cheese is melted and slightly browned.
3. Remove the pan from the air fryer, and let it cool for 2 minutes. Invert the pan before the cheese brittle completely cools but is semi-hardened to allow it to easily slide out of the pan.
4. Let the pan cool another 5 minutes. Break into pieces and serve.

Savory Sausage Balls
Cook time: 8 minutes | Serves 10

- 2 cups all-purpose flour
- 1 tablespoon baking powder
- ½ teaspoon garlic powder
- ¼ teaspoon onion powder
- ½ teaspoon salt
- 3 tablespoons milk
- 2½ cups grated pepper jack cheese
- 1 pound fresh sausage, casing removed

1. Preheat the air fryer to 370°F.
2. In a large bowl, whisk together the flour, baking powder, garlic powder, onion powder, and salt. Add in the milk, grated cheese, and sausage.
3. Using a tablespoon, scoop out the sausage and roll it between your hands to form a rounded ball. You should end up with approximately 32 balls. Place them in the air fryer basket in a single layer and working in batches as necessary.
4. Cook for 8 minutes, or until the outer coating turns light brown.
5. Carefully remove, repeating with the remaining sausage balls.

Chili Corn On The Cob

Cook time: 30 minutes | Serves 4

- Salt and pepper to taste
- ½ tsp smoked paprika
- ¼ tsp chili powder
- 4 ears corn, halved
- 1 tbsp butter, melted
- ¼ cup lime juice
- 1 tsp lime zest
- 1 lime, quartered

1. Preheat air fryer to 400°F.
2. Combine salt, pepper, lime juice, lime zest, paprika, and chili powder in a small bowl.
3. Toss corn and butter in a large bowl, then add the seasonings from the small bowl.
4. Toss until coated. Arrange the corn in a single layer in the frying basket.
5. Air Fry for 10 minutes, then turn the corn.
6. Air Fry for another 8 minutes.
7. Squeeze lime over the corn and serve.

Rich Egg-fried Cauliflower Rice

Cook time: 45 minutes | Serves 4

- 2 ½ cups riced cauliflower
- 2 tsp sesame oil
- 1 green bell pepper, diced
- 1 cup peas
- 1 cup diced carrots
- 2 spring onions
- Salt and pepper to taste
- 1 tbsp tamari sauce
- 2 eggs, scrambled

1. Preheat air fryer to 370°F.
2. Combine riced cauliflower, bell pepper, peas, carrots, and spring onions in a large bowl.
3. Stir in 1 tsp of sesame oil, salt, and pepper.
4. Grease a baking pan with the remaining tsp of sesame oil.
5. Transfer the rice mixture to the pan and place in the air fryer.
6. Bake for 10 minutes.
7. Remove the pan and drizzle with tamari sauce.
8. Stir in scrambled eggs and serve warm. 3

Bacon & Blue Cheese Tartlets

Cook time: 30 minutes | Serves 6

- 6 bacon slices
- 16 phyllo tartlet shells
- ½ cup diced blue cheese
- 3 tbsp apple jelly

1. Preheat the air fryer to 400°F.
2. Put the bacon in a single layer in the frying basket and Air Fry for 14 minutes, turning once halfway through.
3. Remove and drain on paper towels, then crumble when cool.
4. Wipe the fryer clean.
5. Fill the tartlet shells with bacon and the blue cheese cubes and add a dab of apple jelly on top of the filling.
6. Lower the temperature to 350°F, then put the shells in the frying basket.
7. Air Fry until the cheese melts and the shells brown, about 5-6 minutes.
8. Remove and serve.

Spiced Roasted Pepitas

Cook time: 25 minutes | Serves 4

- 2 cups pumpkin seeds
- 1 tbsp butter, melted
- Salt and pepper to taste
- ½ tsp shallot powder
- ½ tsp smoked paprika
- ½ tsp dried parsley
- ½ tsp garlic powder
- ¼ tsp dried chives
- ¼ tsp dry mustard
- ¼ tsp celery seed

1. Preheat air fryer to 325°F.
2. Combine the pumpkin seeds, butter, and salt in a bowl.
3. Place the seed mixture in the frying basket and Roast for 13 minutes, turning once.
4. Transfer to a medium serving bowl.
5. Stir in shallot powder, paprika, parsley, garlic powder, chives, dry mustard, celery seed, and black pepper.
6. Serve right away.

Mozzarella En Carrozza with Puttanesca Sauce

Cook time: 8 minutes | Serves 6

- Puttanesca Sauce
- 2 teaspoons olive oil
- 1 anchovy, chopped (optional)
- 2 cloves garlic, minced
- 1 (14-ounce) can petite diced tomatoes
- ½ cup chicken stock or water
- ⅓ cup Kalamata olives, chopped
- 2 tablespoons capers
- ½ teaspoon dried oregano
- ¼ teaspoon crushed red pepper flakes
- salt and freshly ground black pepper
- 1 tablespoon fresh parsley, chopped
- 8 slices of thinly sliced white bread (Pepperidge Farm®)
- 8 ounces mozzarella cheese, cut into ¼-inch slices
- ½ cup all-purpose flour
- 3 eggs, beaten
- 1½ cups seasoned panko breadcrumbs
- ½ teaspoon garlic powder
- ½ teaspoon salt
- freshly ground black pepper
- olive oil, in a spray bottle

1. Start by making the puttanesca sauce. Heat the olive oil in a medium saucepan on the stovetop. Add the anchovies (if using, and I really think you should!) and garlic and sauté for 3 minutes, or until the anchovies have "melted" into the oil. Add the tomatoes, chicken stock, olives, capers, oregano and crushed red pepper flakes and simmer the sauce for 20 minutes. Season with salt and freshly ground black pepper and stir in the fresh parsley.
2. Cut the crusts off the slices of bread. Place four slices of the bread on a cutting board. Divide the cheese between the four slices of bread. Top the cheese with the remaining four slices of bread to make little sandwiches and cut each sandwich into 4 triangles.
3. Set up a dredging station using three shallow dishes. Place the flour in the first shallow dish, the eggs in the second dish and in the third dish, combine the panko breadcrumbs, garlic powder, salt and black pepper. Dredge each little triangle in the flour first (you might think this is redundant, but it helps to get the coating to adhere to the edges of the sandwiches) and then dip them into the egg, making sure both the sides and the edges are coated. Let the excess egg drip off and then press the triangles into the breadcrumb mixture, pressing the crumbs on with your hands so they adhere. Place the coated triangles in the freezer for 2 hours, until the cheese is frozen.
4. Preheat the air fryer to 390°F. Spray all sides of the mozzarella triangles with oil and transfer a single layer of triangles to the air fryer basket. Air-fry in batches at 390°F for 5 minutes. Turn the triangles over and air-fry for an additional 3 minutes.
5. Serve mozzarella triangles immediately with the warm puttanesca sauce.

Cheeseburger Slider Pockets

Cook time: 13 minutes | Serves 4

- 1 pound extra lean ground beef
- 2 teaspoons steak seasoning
- 2 tablespoons Worcestershire sauce
- 8 ounces Cheddar cheese
- ⅓ cup ketchup
- ¼ cup light mayonnaise
- 1 tablespoon pickle relish
- 1 pound frozen bread dough, defrosted
- 1 egg, beaten
- sesame seeds
- vegetable or olive oil, in a spray bottle

1. Combine the ground beef, steak seasoning and Worcestershire sauce in a large bowl. Divide the meat mixture into 12 equal portions. Cut the Cheddar cheese into twelve 2-inch squares, about ¼-inch thick. Stuff a square of cheese into the center of each portion of meat and shape into a 3-inch patty.
2. Make the slider sauce by combining the ketchup, mayonnaise, and relish in a small bowl. Set aside.
3. Cut the bread dough into twelve pieces. Shape each piece of dough into a ball and use a rolling pin to roll them out into 4-inch circles. Dollop ½ teaspoon of the slider sauce into the center of each dough circle. Place a beef patty on top of the sauce and wrap the dough around the patty, pinching the dough together to seal the pocket shut. Try not to stretch the dough too much when bringing the edges together. Brush both sides of the slider pocket with the beaten egg. Sprinkle sesame seeds on top of each pocket.
4. Preheat the air fryer to 350°F.
5. Spray or brush the bottom of the air fryer basket with oil. Air-fry the slider pockets four at a time. Transfer the slider pockets to the air fryer basket, seam side down and air-fry at 350°F for 10 minutes, until the dough is golden brown. Flip the slider pockets over and air-fry for another 3 minutes. When all the batches are done, pop all the sliders into the air fryer for a few minutes to re-heat and serve them hot out of the fryer.

Crispy Okra Fries

Cook time: 25 minutes | Serves 4

- ½ lb trimmed okra, cut lengthways
- ¼ tsp deggi mirch chili powder
- 3 tbsp buttermilk
- 2 tbsp chickpea flour
- 2 tbsp cornmeal
- Salt and pepper to taste

1. Preheat air fryer to 380°F.
2. Set out 2 bowls. In one, add buttermilk.
3. In the second, mix flour, cornmeal, chili powder, salt, and pepper.
4. Dip the okra in buttermilk, then dredge in flour and cornmeal.
5. Transfer to the frying basket and spray the okra with oil.
6. Air Fry for 10 minutes, shaking once halfway through cooking until crispy.
7. Let cool for a few minutes and serve warm.

Artichoke Samosas

Cook time: 25 minutes | Serves 6

- ½ cup minced artichoke hearts
- ¼ cup ricotta cheese
- 1 egg white
- 3 tbsp grated mozzarella
- ½ tsp dried thyme
- 6 phyllo dough sheets
- 2 tbsp melted butter
- 1 cup mango chutney

1. Preheat air fryer to 400°F. Mix together ricotta cheese, egg white, artichoke hearts, mozzarella cheese, and thyme in a small bowl until well blended. When you bring out the phyllo dough, cover it with a damp kitchen towel so that it doesn't dry out while you are working with it. Take one sheet of phyllo and place it on the work surface.
2. Cut it into thirds lengthwise. At the base of each strip, place about 1 ½ tsp of filling. Fold the bottom right-hand tip of the strip over to the left-hand side to make a triangle. Continue flipping and folding triangles along the strip. Brush the triangle with butter to seal the edges. Place triangles in the greased frying basket and Bake until golden and crisp, 4 minutes. Serve with mango chutney.

Cheesy Spinach Dip
Cook time: 35 minutes | Serves 6

- ½ can refrigerated breadstick dough
- 8 oz feta cheese, cubed
- ¼ cup sour cream
- ½ cup baby spinach
- ½ cup grated Swiss cheese
- 2 green onions, chopped
- 2 tbsp melted butter
- 4 tsp grated Parmesan cheese

1. Preheat air fryer to 320°F. Blend together feta, sour cream, spinach, Swiss cheese, and green onions in a bowl. Spread into the pan and Bake until hot, about 8 minutes. Unroll six of the breadsticks and cut in half crosswise to make 12 pieces. Carefully stretch each piece and tie into a loose knot. Tuck in the ends to prevent burning.
2. When the dip is ready, remove the pan from the air fryer and place each bread knot on top of the dip until the dip is covered. Brush melted butter on each knot and sprinkle with Parmesan. Bake until the knots are golden, 8-13 minutes. Serve warm.

Parmesan Crackers
Cook time: 6 minutes | Serves 6

- 2 cups finely grated Parmesan cheese
- ¼ teaspoon paprika
- ¼ teaspoon garlic powder
- ½ teaspoon dried thyme
- 1 tablespoon all-purpose flour

1. Preheat the air fryer to 380°F.
2. In a medium bowl, stir together the Parmesan, paprika, garlic powder, thyme, and flour.
3. Line the air fryer basket with parchment paper.
4. Using a tablespoon measuring tool, create 1-tablespoon mounds of seasoned cheese on the parchment paper, leaving 2 inches between the mounds to allow for spreading.
5. Cook the crackers for 6 minutes. Allow the cheese to harden and cool before handling. Repeat in batches with the remaining cheese.

Onion Puffs

Cook time: 8 minutes | Serves 14

- Vegetable oil spray
- ¾ cup Chopped yellow or white onion
- ½ cup Seasoned Italian-style panko bread crumbs
- 4½ tablespoons All-purpose flour
- 4½ tablespoons Whole, low-fat, or fat-free milk
- 1½ tablespoons Yellow cornmeal
- 1¼ teaspoons Granulated white sugar
- ½ teaspoon Baking powder
- ¼ teaspoon Table salt

1. Cut or tear a piece of aluminum foil so that it lines the air fryer's basket with a ½-inch space on each of its four sides. Lightly coat the foil with vegetable oil spray, then set the foil sprayed side up inside the basket.
2. Preheat the air fryer to 400°F.
3. Stir the onion, bread crumbs, flour, milk, cornmeal, sugar, baking powder, and salt in a bowl to form a thick batter.
4. Remove the basket from the machine. Drop the onion batter by 2-tablespoon measures onto the foil, spacing the mounds evenly across its surface. Return the basket to the machine and air-fry undisturbed for 4 minutes.
5. Remove the basket from the machine. Lightly coat the puffs with vegetable oil spray. Use kitchen tongs to pick up a corner of the foil, then gently pull it out of the basket, letting the puffs slip onto the basket directly. Return the basket to the machine and continue air-frying undisturbed for 8 minutes, or until brown and crunchy.
6. Use kitchen tongs to transfer the puffs to a wire rack or a serving platter. Cool for 5 minutes before serving.

Crispy Chicken Bites with Gorgonzola Sauce

Cook time: 30 minutes | Serves 4

- ¼ cup crumbled Gorgonzola cheese
- ¼ cup creamy blue cheese salad dressing
- 1 lb chicken tenders, cut into thirds crosswise
- ½ cup sour cream
- 1 celery stalk, chopped
- 3 tbsp buffalo chicken sauce
- 1 cup panko bread crumbs
- 2 tbsp olive oil

1. Preheat air fryer to 350°F. Blend together sour cream, salad dressing, Gorgonzola cheese, and celery in a bowl. Set aside. Combine chicken pieces and Buffalo wing sauce in another bowl until the chicken is coated.
2. In a shallow bowl or pie plate, mix the bread crumbs and olive oil. Dip the chicken into the bread crumb mixture, patting the crumbs to keep them in place. Arrange the chicken in the greased frying basket and Air Fry for 8-9 minutes, shaking once halfway through cooking until the chicken is golden. Serve with the blue cheese sauce.

Chapter 3
Breakfast Recipes

Pumpkin Muffins

Prep time: 15 minutes | Cook time: 13 minutes | Serves 8

- ½ cup pumpkin puree
- 1 cup gluten-free oats
- ¼ cup honey
- 1 medium egg beaten
- ½ teaspoon coconut butter
- ½ tablespoon cocoa nib
- ½ tablespoon vanilla essence
- Cooking spray
- ½ teaspoon nutmeg

1. Add oats, honey, eggs, pumpkin puree, coconut butter, cocoa nibs, vanilla essence, and nutmeg to a bowl and mix well until smooth.
2. Divide the batter into two 4-cup muffin trays, greased with cooking spray.
3. Place one mini muffin tray in each of the two crisper plates.
4. Return the crisper plates to the Ninja Foodi Dual Zone Air Fryer.
5. Choose the Air Fry mode for Zone 1 and set the temperature to 375 degrees F/ 190 degrees C and the time to 13 minutes.
6. Select the "MATCH" button to copy the settings for Zone 2.
7. Initiate cooking by pressing the START/STOP button.
8. Allow the muffins to cool, then serve.

Egg and Avocado in The Ninja Foodi

Prep time: 10 minutes | Cook time: 12 minutes | Serves 2

- 2 avocados, pitted and cut in half
- Garlic salt, to taste
- Cooking oil for greasing
- 4 eggs
- ¼ teaspoon Paprika powder for sprinkling
- ⅓ cup Parmesan cheese, crumbled
- 6 bacon strips, raw

1. First, cut the avocado in half and pit it.
2. Now scoop out the flesh from the avocado and keep aside
3. Crack one egg in each hole of the avocado and sprinkle paprika and garlic salt.
4. Sprinkle it with cheese at the end.
5. Now put it into tin foils and then put it in the air fryer zone basket 1.
6. Put bacon strips in zone 2 basket.
7. Now for zone 1, set it to AIR FRY mode at 350 degrees F/ 175 degrees C for 10 minutes.
8. Place the bacon in zone 2, set it to 400 degrees F/ 200 degrees C for 12 minutes on AIR FRY mode.
9. Press the Sync button and press START/STOP button so it will finish at the same time.
10. Once done, serve and enjoy.

Sweet Potatoes Hash

Prep time: 15 minutes | Cook time: 25 minutes | Serves 2

- 450 grams sweet potatoes
- ½ white onion, diced
- 3 tablespoons olive oil
- 1 teaspoon smoked Paprika
- ¼ teaspoon cumin
- ⅓ teaspoon ground turmeric
- ¼ teaspoon garlic salt
- 1 cup guacamole

1. Peel and cut the potatoes into cubes.
2. Transfer the potatoes to a bowl and add oil, white onions, cumin, Paprika, turmeric, and garlic salt.
3. Put this mixture between both the baskets of the Ninja Foodie 2-Basket Air Fryer.
4. Set zone 1 to AIR FRY mode for 10 minutes at 390 degrees F/ 200 degrees C.
5. Press the MATCH button for zone 2.
6. Take out the baskets and shake them well.
7. Set the timer to 15 minutes at 390 degrees F/ 200 degrees C and AIR FRY again and MATCH for zone 2.
8. Once done, serve it with guacamole.

Bacon and Egg Omelet

Prep time: 12 minutes | Cook time: 10 minutes | Serves 2

- 2 eggs, whisked
- ½ teaspoon chopped tomatoes
- Sea salt and black pepper, to taste
- 2 teaspoons almond milk
- 1 teaspoon cilantro, chopped
- 1 small green chili, chopped
- 4 strips bacon

1. Take a bowl and whisk the eggs in it.
2. Then add the green chili, salt, black pepper, cilantro, almond milk, and chopped tomatoes.
3. Grease the ramekins with.
4. Pour this into ramekins.
5. Put the bacon in the zone 1 basket and ramekins in zone 2 basket of the Ninja Foodi2-Basket Air Fryer.
6. Now for zone 1, set it to AIR FRY mode at 400 degrees F/ 200 degrees C for 10 minutes.
7. For zone 2, set it to 350 degrees F/ 175 degrees Cor 10 minutes in AIR FRY mode.
8. Press theSync button and press START/STOP button so thatit will finish both at the same time.
9. Once done, serve and enjoy.

Yellow Potatoes with Eggs

Prep time: 10 minutes | Cook time: 35 minutes | Serves 2

- 1 pound of Dutch yellow potatoes, quartered
- 1 red bell pepper, chopped
- Salt and black pepper, to taste
- 1 green bell pepper, chopped
- 2 teaspoons olive oil
- 2 teaspoons garlic powder
- 1 teaspoon onion powder
- 1 egg
- ¼ teaspoon butter

1. Toss together diced potatoes, green pepper, red pepper, salt, black pepper, and olive oil along with garlic powder and onion powder.
2. Put the potatoes in the zone 1 basket of the air fryer.
3. Take a ramekin and grease it with oil spray.
4. Whisk the egg in a bowl and add salt and pepper along with ½ teaspoon of butter.
5. Pour the egg into the ramekin and place it in the zone 2 basket.
6. Set the timer for zone 1 basket to 30-35 minutes at 400 degrees F/ 200 degrees C at AIR FRY mode.
7. Now for zone 2, set it to AIR FRY mode at 350 degrees F/ 175 degrees C for 8-10 minutes.
8. Press the Sync button and press START/STOP button so both will finish at the same time.
9. Once done, serve and enjoy.

Egg with Baby Spinach

Prep time: 12 minutes | Cook time: 12 minutes | Serves 4

- Nonstick spray, for greasing ramekins
- 2 tablespoons olive oil
- 6 ounces baby spinach
- 2 garlic cloves, minced
- ⅓ teaspoon kosher salt
- 6-8 large eggs
- ½ cup half and half
- Salt and black pepper, to taste
- 8 Sourdough bread slices, toasted

1. Grease 4 ramekins with oil spray and set them aside for further use.
2. Take a skillet and heat oil in it.
3. Cook spinach for 2 minutes and add the garlic, salt and black pepper.
4. Let it simmer for 2 more minutes.
5. Once the spinach is wilted, transfer it to a plate.
6. Whisk the eggs in a small bowl.
7. Add in the spinach.
8. Whisk it well and then pour in the half and half.
9. Divide this mixture between 4 ramekins and remember not to overfill it to the top.
10. Put the ramekins in zone 1 and zone 2 baskets of the Ninja Foodie 2-Basket Air Fryer.
11. Press START/STOP button and set zone 1 to AIR FRY at 350 degrees F/ 175 degrees C for 8-12 minutes.
12. Press the MATCH button for zone 2.
13. Once it's cooked and eggs are done, serve with sourdough bread slices.

Banana and Raisins Muffins

Prep time: 20 minutes | Cook time: 16 minutes | Serves 2

- Salt, pinch
- 2 eggs, whisked
- ⅓ cup butter, melted
- 4 tablespoons almond milk
- ¼ teaspoon vanilla extract
- ½ teaspoon baking powder
- 1-½ cup all-purpose flour
- 1 cup mashed bananas
- 2 tablespoons raisins

1. Take about 4 large (one-cup sized) ramekins and layer them with muffin papers.
2. Crack the eggs in a large bowl, and whisk it all well and addvanilla extract, almond milk, baking powder, and melted butter.
3. Whisk the ingredients in very well.
4. Take a separate bowl and add the all-purpose flour and salt.
5. Combine the dry ingredients with the wet ingredients.
6. Pour mashed bananas and raisins into the batter.
7. Mix it well to make a batter for the muffins.
8. Pour the batter into the four ramekins and divide the ramekins into the air fryer zones.
9. Set the timer for zone 1 to 16 minutes at 350 degrees F/ 175 degrees C on AIR FRY mode.
10. Select the MATCH button for the zone 2 basket.
11. Check and if not done, and let it AIR FRY for one more minute.
12. Once it is done, serve.

Bacon and Eggs for Breakfast

Prep time: 12 minutes | Cook time: 12 minutes | Serves 1

- 4 strips of thick-sliced bacon
- 2 small eggs
- Salt and black pepper, to taste
- Oil spray for greasing ramekins

1. Take 2 ramekins and grease them with oil spray.
2. Crack eggs into a bowl and season with salt and black pepper.
3. Divide the egg mixture between the two ramekins.
4. Put the bacon slices into the Ninja Foodie 2-Basket Air Fryer zone 1 basket, and the ramekins in zone 2 basket.
5. Now for zone 1 set it to AIR FRY mode at 400 degrees F/ 200 degrees C for 12 minutes.
6. For zone 2 set it to 350 degrees F/ 175 degrees C for 8 minutes using AIR FRY mode.
7. Press the Syncbutton and press START/STOP button so they both finish at the same time.
8. Once done, serve and enjoy.

Sweet Potato Sausage Hash

Prep time: 10 minutes | Cook time: 20 minutes | Serves 4

- 1½ pounds sweet potato, peeled and diced into ½-inch pieces
- 1 tablespoon minced garlic
- 1 teaspoon kosher salt plus more, as desired
- Ground black pepper, as desired
- 2 tablespoons canola oil
- 1 tablespoon dried sage
- 1-pound uncooked mild ground breakfast sausage
- ½ large onion, peeled and diced
- ½ teaspoon ground cinnamon
- 1 teaspoon chili powder
- 4 large eggs, poached or fried (optional)

1. Toss the sweet potatoes with the garlic, salt, pepper, and canola oil in a mixing bowl.
2. Install the crisper plate in the zone 1 drawer, fill it with the sweet potato mixture, and insert the drawer in the unit.
3. Place the ground sausage in the zone 2 drawer (without the crisper plate) and place it in the unit.
4. Select zone 1, then AIR FRY, and set the temperature to 400 degrees F/ 200 degrees C with a 30-minute timer.
5. Select zone 2, then ROAST, then set the temperature to 400 degrees F/ 200 degrees C with a 20-minute timer. SYNC is the option to choose. To begin cooking, press the START/STOP button.
6. When the zone 1 and zone 2 times have reached 10 minutes, press START/STOP and remove the drawers from the unit. Shake each for 10 seconds.
7. Half of the sage should be added to the zone 1 drawer.
8. Add the onion to the zone 2 drawer and mix to incorporate. To continue cooking, press START/STOP and reinsert the drawers.
9. Remove both drawers from the unit once the cooking is finished and add the potatoes to the sausage mixture. Mix in the cinnamon, sage, chili powder, and salt until thoroughly combined.
10. When the hash is done, stir it and serve it right away with a poached or fried egg on top, if desired.

Air Fried Bacon and Eggs

Prep time: 5 minutes | Cook time: 10 minutes | Serves 1

- 2 eggs
- 2 slices bacon

1. Grease a ramekin using cooking spray.
2. Install the crisper plate in the zone 1 drawer and place the bacon inside it. Insert the drawer into the unit.
3. Crack the eggs and add them to the greased ramekin.
4. Install the crisper plate in the zone 2 drawer and place the ramekin inside it. Insert the drawer into the unit.
5. Select zone 1 to AIR FRY for 9–11 minutes at 400 degrees F/ 200 degrees C. Select zone 2 to AIR FRY for 8–9 minutes at 350 degrees F/ 175 degrees C. Press SYNC.
6. Press START/STOP to begin cooking.
7. Enjoy!

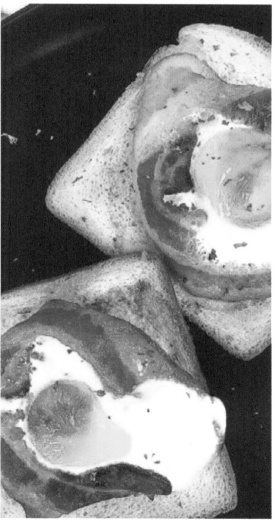

Air Fryer Sausage Patties

Prep time: 5 minutes | Cook time: 10 minutes | Serves 12

- 1-pound pork sausage or ready-made patties
- Fennel seeds or preferred seasonings

1. Prepare the sausage by slicing it into patties, then flavor it with fennel seed or your favorite seasonings.
2. Install a crisper plate in both drawers. Place half the patties in zone 1 and half in zone 2, then insert the drawers into the unit.
3. Select zone 1, select AIR FRY, set temperature to 390 degrees F/ 200 degrees C, and set time to 10 minutes.
4. Select MATCH to match zone 2 settings to zone 1.
5. Press the START/STOP button to begin cooking.
6. When cooking is complete, remove the patties from the unit and serve with sauce or make a burger.

Hash Browns

Prep time: 5 minutes | Cook time: 5 minutes | Serves 4

- 4 frozen hash browns patties
- Cooking oil spray of choice

1. Install a crisper plate in both drawers. Place half the hash browns in zone 1 and half in zone 2, then insert the drawers into the unit. Spray the hash browns with some cooking oil.
2. Select zone 1, select AIR FRY, set temperature to 390 degrees F/ 200 degrees C, and set time to 5 minutes.
3. Select MATCH to match zone 2 settings to zone 1. Press the START/STOP button to begin cooking.
4. When cooking is complete, remove the hash browns and serve.

Egg White Muffins

Prep time: 15 minutes | Cook time: 10 minutes | Serves 8

- 4 slices center-cut bacon, cut into strips
- 4 ounces baby bella mushrooms, roughly chopped
- 2 ounces sun-dried tomatoes
- 2 tablespoon sliced black olives
- 2 tablespoons grated or shredded parmesan
- 2 tablespoons shredded mozzarella
- ¼ teaspoon black pepper
- ¾ cup liquid egg whites
- 2 tablespoons liquid egg whites

1. Heat a saucepan with a little oil, add the bacon and mushrooms and cook until fully cooked and crispy, about 6–8 minutes.
2. While the bacon and mushrooms cook, mix the ¾ cup liquid egg whites, sun-dried tomato, olives, parmesan, mozzarella, and black pepper together in a large bowl.
3. Add the cooked bacon and mushrooms to the tomato and olive mixture, stirring everything together.
4. Spoon the mixture into muffin molds, followed by 2 tablespoons of egg whites over the top.
5. Place half the muffins mold in zone 1 and half in zone 2, then insert the drawers into the unit.
6. Select zone 1, select AIR FRY, set temperature to 390 degrees F/ 200 degrees C, and set time to 22 minutes.
7. Select MATCH to match zone 2 settings to zone 1. Press the START/STOP button to begin cooking.
8. When cooking is complete, remove the molds and enjoy!

Perfect Cinnamon Toast

Prep time: 5 minutes | Cook time: 10 minutes | Serves 6

- 12 slices whole-wheat bread
- 1 stick butter, room temperature
- ½ cup white sugar
- 1½ teaspoons ground cinnamon
- 1½ teaspoons pure vanilla extract
- 1 pinch kosher salt
- 2 pinches freshly ground black pepper (optional)

1. Mash the softened butter with a fork or the back of a spoon in a bowl. Add the sugar, cinnamon, vanilla, and salt. Stir until everything is well combined.
2. Spread one-sixth of the mixture onto each slice of bread, making sure to cover the entire surface.
3. Install a crisper plate in both drawers. Place half the bread sliced in the zone 1 drawer and half in the zone 2 drawer, then insert the drawers into the unit.
4. Select zone 1, select AIR FRY, set temperature to 400 degrees F/ 200 degrees C, and set time to 5 minutes. Select MATCH to match zone 2 settings to zone 1. Press theSTART/STOP button to begin cooking.
5. When cooking is complete, remove the slices and cut them diagonally.
6. Serve immediately.

Bagels

Prep time: 10 minutes | Cook time: 15 minutes | Serves 8

- 2 cups self-rising flour
- 2 cups non-fat plain Greek yogurt
- 2 beaten eggs for egg wash (optional)
- ½ cup sesame seeds (optional)

1. In a medium mixing bowl, combine the self-rising flour and Greek yogurt using a wooden spoon.
2. Knead the dough for about 5 minutes on a lightly floured board.
3. Divide the dough into four equal pieces and roll each into a thin rope, securing the ends to form a bagel shape.
4. Install a crisper plate in both drawers. Place 4 bagels in a single layer in each drawer. Insert the drawers into the unit.
5. Select zone 1, select AIR FRY, set temperature to 360 degrees F/ 180 degrees C, and set time to 15 minutes. Select MATCH to match zone 2 settings to zone 1. Select START/STOP to begin.
6. Once the timer has finished, remove the bagels from the units.
7. Serve and enjoy!

Banana Muffins

Prep time: 5 minutes | Cook time: 15 minutes | Serves 10

- 2 very ripe bananas
- ⅓ cup olive oil
- 1 egg
- ½ cup brown sugar
- 1 teaspoon vanilla extract
- 1 teaspoon cinnamon
- ¾ cup self-rising flour

1. In a large mixing bowl, mash the bananas, then add the egg, brown sugar, olive oil, and vanilla. To blend, stir everything together thoroughly.
2. Fold in the flour and cinnamon until everything is just blended.
3. Fill muffin molds evenly with the mixture (silicone or paper).
4. Install a crisper plate in both drawers. Place the muffin molds in a single layer in each drawer. Insert the drawers into the unit.
5. Select zone 1, select AIR FRY, set temperature to 360 degrees F/ 180 degrees C, and set time to 15 minutes. Select MATCH to match zone 2 settings to zone 1. Select START/STOP to begin.
6. Once the timer has finished, remove the muffins from the drawers.
7. Serve and enjoy!

Donuts

Prep time: 5 minutes | Cook time: 15 minutes | Serves 6

- 1 cup granulated sugar
- 2 tablespoons ground cinnamon
- 1 can refrigerated flaky buttermilk biscuits
- ¼ cup unsalted butter, melted

1. Combine the sugar and cinnamon in a small shallow bowl and set aside.
2. Remove the biscuits from the can and put them on a chopping board, separated. Cut holes in the center of each biscuit with a 1-inch round biscuit cutter (or a similarly sized bottle cap).
3. Place a crisper plate in each drawer. In each drawer, place 4 biscuits in a single layer. Insert the drawers into the unit.
4. Select zone 1, then AIR FRY, then set the temperature to 360 degrees F/ 180 degrees C with a 10-minute timer. To match zone 2 settings to zone 1, choose MATCH. To begin cooking, select START/STOP.
5. Remove the donuts from the drawers after the timer has finished.

Chapter 4
Poultry Mains Recipes

Fajita Stuffed Chicken

Prep time: 10 minutes | Cook time:15 minutes |Serves 2

- 2 boneless skinless chicken breast halves
- ½ onion, thinly sliced
- ½ teaspoon ground cumin
- ½ teaspoon chili powder
- ½ tablespoon olive oil
- ¼ medium green pepper, thinly sliced
- ¼ teaspoon salt
- ⅛ teaspoon garlic powder
- 50g cheddar cheese, cut into slices

1. Cut each chicken breast in the thickest part and fill with green peppers and onion.
2. In a small bowl, combine olive oil and seasonings.
3. Rub over chicken.
4. Grease basket of Ninja Foodi 2-Basket Air Fryer.
5. Press your chosen zone - "Zone 1" or "Zone 2" and then rotate the knob to select "Air Fry".
6. Set the heat to 190 degrees C and then set the time for 5 minutes to preheat.
7. After preheating, arrange chicken breasts into the basket of each zone.
8. Slide the basket into the Air Fryer and set the time for 15 minutes.
9. After cooking time is completed, remove the chicken breasts from Air Fryer and serve hot.

Almond Chicken

Prep time: 15 minutes | Cook time:30 minutes |Serves 2

- 2 chicken breast halves, boneless and skinless
- 2 small eggs
- 1 teaspoon garlic salt
- 4 tablespoons buttermilk
- 70g silvered almonds, finely chopped
- ½ teaspoon pepper

1. Take a shallow bowl, whisk egg, buttermilk, pepper and garlic salt.
2. Place almonds in another shallow bowl.
3. Dip chicken breasts into the egg mixture and then coat with almonds.
4. Grease basket of Ninja Foodi 2-Basket Air Fryer.
5. Press your chosen zone - "Zone 1" or "Zone 2" and then rotate the knob to select "Air Fry".
6. Set the temperature to 175 degrees C and then set the time for 5 minutes to preheat.
7. After preheating, arrange the chicken into the basket of each zone.
8. Slide the basket into the Air Fryer and set the time for 15 to 18 minutes.
9. After cooking time is completed, remove chicken from Air Fryer and serve hot.

Bagel Chicken Strips

Prep time: 8 minutes | Cook time:15 minutes |Serves 2

- 225g chicken tenderloins
- Bagel, torn
- 25g grated Parmesan cheese
- 25g panko breadcrumbs
- 30g butter, cubed
- ⅛ teaspoon crushed red pepper flakes
- ¼ teaspoon salt

1. Take a food processor, pulse torn bagel until crumbs are formed.
2. Place breadcrumbs in a shallow dish and add panko, cheese and pepper flakes.
3. Take another shallow bowl, microwave butter until melted.
4. Sprinkle chicken with salt.
5. Dip chicken in butter, then coat with crumb mixture.
6. Grease basket of Ninja Foodi 2-Basket Air Fryer.
7. Press your chosen zone - "Zone 1" or "Zone 2" and then rotate the knob to select "Air Fry".
8. Set the heat to 200 degrees C and then set the time for 5 minutes to preheat.
9. After preheating, arrange chicken tenderloins into the basket of each zone.
10. Slide the basket into the Air Fryer and set the time for 7 minutes.
11. While cooking, flip the chicken once halfway through.
12. After cooking time is completed, remove the chicken from Air Fryer and serve hot.

Crispy Curry Drumsticks

Prep time: 30 minutes | Cook time:15 minutes |Serves 2

- 225g chicken drumsticks
- 1 tablespoon olive oil
- ½ teaspoon salt, divided
- ¼ teaspoon garlic powder
- ¼ teaspoon onion salt
- 1 teaspoon curry powder

1. In a large bowl, place chicken and add salt and enough water to cover.
2. Let it sit for 15 minutes at room temperature.
3. Drain and pat dry.
4. In another bowl, mix together oil, curry powder, garlic powder, onion salt and remaining salt.
5. Add chicken into the mixture and toss to coat well.
6. Grease basket of Ninja Foodi 2-Basket Air Fryer.
7. Press your chosen zone - "Zone 1" or "Zone 2" and then rotate the knob to select "Air Fry".
8. Set the heat to 190 degrees C and then set the time for 5 minutes to preheat.
9. After preheating, arrange drumsticks into the basket of each zone.
10. Slide the basket into the Air Fryer and set the time for 15 to 17 minutes.
11. While cooking, flip the drumsticks once halfway through.
12. After cooking time is completed, remove the drumsticks from Air Fryer and serve hot.

Chicken Cordon Bleu

Prep time: 15 minutes | Cook time:30 minutes |Serves 4

- 4 (150g) boneless, skinless chicken breast halves, pounded into ½ cm thickness
- 4 (20g) deli ham slices
- 4 Swiss cheese slices
- 125g plain flour
- ¼ teaspoon paprika
- Salt and ground black pepper, as required
- 2 large eggs
- 4 tablespoons 2% milk
- 100g seasoned breadcrumbs
- 2 tablespoons olive oil
- 2 tablespoons butter, melted

1. Arrange the chicken breast halves onto a smooth surface.
2. Arrange 1 ham slice over each chicken breast half, followed by the cheese.
3. Roll up each chicken breast half and tuck in ends.
4. With toothpicks, secure the rolls.
5. In a shallow plate, mix together the flour, paprika, salt and black pepper.
6. In a shallow bowl, place the egg and milk and beat slightly.
7. In a second shallow plate, place the breadcrumbs.
8. Coat each chicken roll with flour mixture, then dip into egg mixture and finally coat with breadcrumbs.
9. In a small frying pan, heat the oil over medium heat and cook the chicken rolls for about 3-5 minutes or until browned from all sides.
10. Grease basket of Ninja Foodi 2-Basket Air Fryer.
11. Press your chosen zone - "Zone 1" or "Zone 2" and then rotate the knob to select "Bake".
12. Set the temperature to 175 degrees C and then set the time for 5 minutes to preheat.
13. After preheating, arrange the 2 chicken rolls into the basket of each zone.
14. Slide the basket into the Air Fryer and set the time for 25 minutes.
15. After cooking time is completed, remove the baking pan of chicken from Air Fryer.
16. Transfer the chicken rolls onto a platter and discard the toothpicks.
17. Drizzle with melted butter and serve.

Chicken Parmesan

Prep time: 10 minutes | Cook time:20 minutes |Serves 2

- 2 boneless skinless chicken breast halves
- 25g breadcrumbs
- 25g grated Parmesan cheese
- 1 egg
- ⅛ teaspoon pepper
- 110g shredded mozzarella cheese
- 120g pasta sauce

1. In a shallow bowl, beat egg.
2. Take another bowl, add breadcrumbs, Parmesan cheese and pepper.
3. Dip chicken breast in egg and then coat with breadcrumbs mixture.
4. Grease basket of Ninja Foodi 2-Basket Air Fryer.
5. Press your chosen zone - "Zone 1" or "Zone 2" and then rotate the knob to select "Air Fry".
6. Set the heat to 190 degrees C and then set the time for 5 minutes to preheat.
7. After preheating, arrange chicken breast halves into the basket of each zone.
8. Slide the basket into the Air Fryer and set the time for 10 to 12 minutes.
9. While cooking, flip the chicken once halfway through and top with sauce and cheese.
10. After cooking time is completed, remove the chicken thighs from Air Fryer and serve hot.

Thyme Duck Breast

Prep time: 10 minutes | Cook time:15 minutes |Serves 4

- 480ml beer
- 2 tablespoons olive oil
- 2 teaspoons mustard
- 2 tablespoons fresh thyme, chopped
- Salt and ground black pepper, as required
- 2 (250g) duck breasts

1. In a bowl, place the beer, oil, mustard, thyme, salt, and black pepper and mix well
2. Add the duck breasts and coat with marinade generously.
3. Cover and refrigerate for about 4 hours.
4. Remove from the refrigerator and with a piece of foil, cover each duck breast.
5. Press "Zone 1" of Ninja Foodi 2-Basket Air Fryer and then rotate the knob for each zone to select "Air Fry".
6. Set the temperature to 200 degrees C and then set the time for 5 minutes to preheat.
7. After preheating, arrange 1 covered duck breast into the basket of each zone.
8. Slide the basket into the Air Fryer and set the time for 15 minutes.
9. After 5 minutes of cooking, remove the foil from duck breast and set the temperature to 180 degrees C.
10. After cooking time is completed, remove the duck breast from Air Fryer.

11. Place the duck breasts onto a cutting board for about 5 minutes before slicing.
12. With a sharp knife, cut each duck breast into desired size slices and serve.

Spicy Roasted Chicken

Prep time: 15 minutes | Cook time: 1 hour 10 minutes |Serves 12

- 115g butter, softened
- 4 teaspoons dried rosemary
- 4 teaspoons dried thyme
- 2 tablespoons Cajun seasoning
- 2 tablespoons onion powder
- 2 tablespoons garlic powder
- 2 tablespoons paprika
- 2 teaspoons cayenne pepper
- Salt, as required
- 2 (1.4kg) whole chicken, neck and giblets removed

1. In a bowl, add the butter, herbs, spices and salt and mix well.
2. Rub each chicken with spice mixture generously.
3. With kitchen twine, tie off the wings and legs of each chicken.
4. Grease basket of Ninja Foodi 2-Basket Air Fryer.
5. Press your chosen zone - "Zone 1" or "Zone 2" and then rotate the knob to select "Bake".
6. Set the temperature to 180 degrees C and then set the time for 5 minutes to preheat.
7. After preheating, arrange 1 chicken into the basket of each zone.
8. Slide the basket into the Air Fryer and set the time for 70 minutes.
9. After cooking time is completed, remove the chickens from Air Fryer and place each onto a platter for about 10 minutes before serving.
10. Cut each chicken into desired-sized pieces and serve.

Marinated Chicken Legs

Prep time: 15 minutes | Cook time: 20 minutes | Serves 4

- 4 (200g) chicken legs
- 2 tablespoons balsamic vinegar
- 2 teaspoons garlic, minced
- Salt, as required
- 4 tablespoons plain Greek yogurt
- 1 teaspoon red chili powder
- 1 teaspoon ground cumin
- 1 teaspoon ground coriander
- Ground black pepper, as required

1. In a bowl, add the chicken legs, vinegar, garlic and salt and mix well.
2. Set aside for about 15 minutes.
3. Meanwhile, in another bowl, mix together the yogurt, spices, salt and black pepper.
4. Add the chicken legs into the bowl and coat with the spice mixture generously.
5. Grease basket of Ninja Foodi 2-Basket Air Fryer.
6. Press your chosen zone - "Zone 1" or "Zone 2" and then rotate the knob to select "Air Fry".
7. Set the temperature to 200 degrees C and then set the time for 5 minutes to preheat.
8. After preheating, arrange 2 chicken legs into the basket of each zone.
9. Slide the basket into the Air Fryer and set the time for 20 minutes.
10. After cooking time is completed, remove the chicken legs from Air Fryer and serve hot.

Spicy Chicken Thighs

Prep time: 10 minutes | Cook time: 20 minutes | Serves 8

- 2 teaspoons ground cumin
- 2 teaspoons garlic powder
- 1 teaspoon smoked paprika
- 1 teaspoon ground coriander
- Salt and ground black pepper, as required
- 8 (125g) chicken thighs
- 4 tablespoons olive oil

1. In a large bowl, add the spices, salt and black pepper and mix well.
2. Coat the chicken thighs with oil and then rub with spice mixture.
3. Grease basket of Ninja Foodi 2-Basket Air Fryer.
4. Press your chosen zone - "Zone 1" or "Zone 2" and then rotate the knob to select "Air Fry".
5. Set the temperature to 200 degrees C and then set the time for 5 minutes to preheat.
6. After preheating, arrange 4 chicken thighs into the basket of each zone.
7. Slide the basket into the Air Fryer and set the time for 20 minutes.
8. While cooking, flip the chicken thighs once halfway through.
9. After cooking time is completed, remove the chicken thighs from Air Fryer and serve hot.

Crispy Chicken Breasts

Prep time: 15 minutes | Cook time: 40 minutes | Serves 6

- 60g flour
- 2 large eggs, beaten
- 10g fresh coriander, chopped
- 80g croutons, crushed
- 6 (125g) boneless, skinless chicken breasts

1. In a shallow, dish place the flour.
2. In a second shallows dish, mix together the egg and coriander.
3. In a third shallow dish, place croutons.
4. Coat the chicken breasts with flour, then dip into eggs and finally coat with croutons.
5. Grease basket of Ninja Foodi 2-Basket Air Fryer.
6. Press your chosen zone - "Zone 1" or "Zone 2" and then rotate the knob to select "Bake".
7. Set the temperature to 190 degrees C and then set the time for 5 minutes to preheat.
8. After preheating, arrange 3 chicken breasts into the basket of each zone.
9. Slide the basket into the Air Fryer and set the time for 40 minutes.
10. While cooking, flip the chicken breasts once halfway through.
11. After cooking time is completed, remove the chicken breasts from Air Fryer and serve hot.

Stuffed Chicken Breasts

Prep time: 15 minutes | Cook time: 30 minutes | Serves 4

- 2 tablespoon olive oil
- 85g fresh spinach
- 125g ricotta cheese, shredded
- 4 (100g) skinless, boneless chicken breasts
- Salt and ground black pepper, as required
- 4 tablespoons Parmesan cheese, grated
- ½ teaspoon paprika

1. In a medium frying pan, heat the oil over medium heat and cook the spinach for about 3-4 minutes.
2. Stir in the ricotta and cook for about 40-60 seconds.
3. Remove the frying pan from heat and set aside to cool.
4. Cut slits into the chicken breasts about ½ cm apart but not all the way through.
5. Season each chicken breast with salt and black pepper and then sprinkle the top with Parmesan cheese and paprika.
6. Grease basket of Ninja Foodi 2-Basket Air Fryer.
7. Press your chosen zone - "Zone 1" or "Zone 2" and then rotate the knob to select "Air Fry".
8. Set the temperature to 200 degrees C and then set the time for 5 minutes to preheat.
9. After preheating, arrange 2 chicken breasts into the basket of each zone.
10. Slide the basket into the Air Fryer and set the time for 25 minutes.
11. After cooking time is completed, remove the chicken breasts from Air Fryer and serve hot.

Gingered Chicken Drumsticks

Prep time: 10 minutes | Cook time: 25 minutes |Serves 6

- 120ml full-fat coconut milk
- 4 teaspoons fresh ginger, minced
- 4 teaspoons galangal, minced
- 2 teaspoons ground turmeric
- Salt, as required
- 6 (150g) chicken drumsticks

1. In a large bowl, place the coconut milk, galangal, ginger, and spices and mix well.
2. Add the chicken drumsticks and coat with the marinade generously.
3. Refrigerate to marinate for at least 6-8 hours.
4. Grease basket of Ninja Foodi 2-Basket Air Fryer.
5. Press your chosen zone - "Zone 1" or "Zone 2" and then rotate the knob to select "Air Fry".
6. Set the temperature to 190 degrees C and then set the time for 5 minutes to preheat.
7. After preheating, arrange 3 drumsticks into the basket of each zone.
8. Slide the basket into the Air Fryer and set the time for 25 minutes.
9. After cooking time is completed, remove the drumsticks from Air Fryer and serve hot.

Glazed Chicken Drumsticks

Prep time: 10 minutes | Cook time: 20 minutes |Serves 4

- 60g Dijon mustard
- 1 tablespoon honey
- 2 tablespoons rapeseed oil
- 1 tablespoon fresh parsley, minced
- Salt and ground black pepper, as required
- 4 (150g) chicken drumsticks

1. In a bowl, add all ingredients except the drumsticks and mix until well combined.
2. Add the drumsticks and coat with the mixture generously.
3. Cover the bowl and place in the refrigerator to marinate overnight.
4. Grease either basket of "Zone 1" or "Zone 2" of Ninja Foodi 2-Basket Air Fryer.
5. Press your chosen zone - "Zone 1" or "Zone 2" and then rotate the knob to select "Air Fry".
6. Set the temperature to 160 degrees C and then set the time for 5 minutes to preheat.
7. After preheating, arrange drumsticks into the basket.
8. Slide basket into Air Fryer and set the time for 12 minutes.
9. After 12 minutes, flip the drumsticks and set the temperature to 200 degrees C.
10. Set the time for 8 minutes.
11. After cooking time is completed, remove the drumsticks from Air Fryer and serve hot.

Sweet Potato-Crusted Chicken Nuggets

Prep time: 10 minutes | Cook time: 10 minutes |Serves 2

- 225g chicken tenderloins, cut into pieces
- ½ tablespoon cornflour
- 50g sweet potato chips
- ½ teaspoon salt, divided
- 2 tablespoons plain flour
- ¼ teaspoon coarsely ground pepper
- ⅛ teaspoon baking powder

1. In a food processor, add chips, pepper, salt and baking powder. Pulse until ground.
2. Transfer to a shallow bowl.
3. Take a bowl, mix cornflour and remaining salt.
4. Place the chicken in the cornflour mixture and then toss with potato chip mixture.
5. Grease basket of Ninja Foodi 2-Basket Air Fryer.
6. Press your chosen zone - "Zone 1" or "Zone 2" and then rotate the knob to select "Air Fry".
7. Set the temperature to 200 degrees C and then set the time for 5 minutes to preheat.
8. After preheating, arrange chicken nuggets into the basket of each zone.
9. Slide the basket into the Air Fryer and set the time for 10 minutes.
10. After cooking time is completed, remove the chicken nuggets from Air Fryer and serve hot.

Southern Style Chicken

Prep time: 10 minutes | Cook time: 20 minutes |Serves 6

- 900g chicken, cut up
- 85g crushed Ritz crackers
- ½ teaspoon paprika
- ½ teaspoon garlic salt
- ½ tablespoon minced fresh parsley
- ⅛ teaspoon rubbed sage
- ⅛ teaspoon ground cumin
- ¼ teaspoon pepper
- 1 small egg, beaten

1. Take a bowl, add all ingredients except chicken and egg. Mix well.
2. Take another bowl and whisk egg.
3. Dip chicken in egg, then coat with cracker mixture.
4. Grease basket of Ninja Foodi 2-Basket Air Fryer.
5. Press your chosen zone - "Zone 1" or "Zone 2" and then rotate the knob to select "Air Fry".
6. Set the heat to 190 degrees C and then set the time for 5 minutes to preheat.
7. After preheating, arrange chicken into the basket of each zone.
8. Slide the basket into the Air Fryer and set the time for 15 to 20 minutes.
9. After cooking time is completed, remove the chicken from Air Fryer and place onto a platter.
10. Serve and enjoy.

Simple Chicken Thighs

Prep time: 10 minutes | Cook time: 20 minutes |Serves 8

- 8 (100g) skinless, boneless chicken thighs
- Salt and ground black pepper, as required
- 4 tablespoons butter, melted

1. Line each basket of "Zone 1" and "Zone 2" of Ninja Foodi 2-Basket Air Fryer with a lightly greased square piece of foil.
2. Press your chosen zone - "Zone 1" or "Zone 2" and then rotate the knob to select "Roast".
3. Set the temperature to 230 degrees C and then set the time for 5 minutes to preheat.
4. Meanwhile, rub the chicken thighs with salt and black pepper evenly and then brush with melted butter.
5. After preheating, arrange 4 chicken thighs into the basket of each zone.
6. Slide the basket into the Air Fryer and set the time for 20 minutes.
7. After cooking time is completed, remove the chicken thighs from Air Fryer.
8. Serve hot.

Simple Turkey Breast

Prep time: 10 minutes | Cook time: 20 minutes |Serves 12

- 2 (1.2kg) bone-in, skin-on turkey breast half
- Salt and ground black pepper, as required

1. Rub the turkey breast with the salt and black pepper evenly.
2. Grease basket of Ninja Foodi 2-Basket Air Fryer.
3. Press your chosen zone - "Zone 1" or "Zone 2" and then rotate the knob to select "Bake".
4. Set the temperature to 200 degrees C and then set the time for 5 minutes to preheat.
5. After preheating, arrange 1 turkey breast into the basket of each zone.
6. Slide the basket into the Air Fryer and set the time for 80 minutes.
7. After cooking time is completed, remove the turkey breasts from Air Fryer and place onto a platter.
8. With a piece of foil, cover each turkey breast for about 20 minutes before slicing.
9. With a sharp knife, cut each turkey breast into desired size slices and serve.

Lemon Feta Chicken

Prep time: 15 minutes | Cook time: 25 minutes |Serves 2

- 2 chicken breast halves, boneless and skinless
- 2 tablespoons crumbled feta cheese
- ½ teaspoon dried oregano
- ¼ teaspoon pepper
- 2 tablespoons lemon juice

1. Take a baking dish, place chicken and pour lemon juice over chicken.
2. Sprinkle with feta cheese, oregano and pepper.
3. Press "Zone 1" of Ninja Foodi 2-Basket Air Fryer and then rotate the knob for each zone to select "Air Fry".
4. Set the heat to 200 degrees C and then set the time for 5 minutes to preheat.
5. After preheating, arrange chicken into the basket of each zone.
6. Slide the basket into the Air Fryer and set the time for 20 to 25 minutes.
7. After cooking time is completed, remove the chicken breast from Air Fryer.
8. Serve and enjoy.

Buffalo Chicken

Prep time: 10 minutes | Cook time: 16 minutes |Serves 2

- 225g chicken breasts, skinless and boneless
- ½ tablespoon cayenne pepper
- ½ tablespoon garlic pepper seasoning
- ½ tablespoon sweet paprika
- ½ teaspoon hot sauce
- 55g panko breadcrumbs
- 2 tablespoons egg substitute
- 60g plain fat-free Greek yogurt

1. In a bowl, whisk Greek yogurt, egg substitute and hot sauce.
2. Take another bowl, mix panko breadcrumbs, paprika, garlic pepper and cayenne pepper.
3. Dip chicken strips into yogurt mixture and then coat with panko breadcrumb mixture.
4. Grease basket of Ninja Foodi 2-Basket Air Fryer.
5. Press your chosen zone - "Zone 1" or "Zone 2" and then rotate the knob to select "Air Fry".
6. Set the temperature to 200 degrees C and then set the time for 5 minutes to preheat.
7. After preheating, arrange coated chicken into the basket of each zone.
8. Slide the basket into the Air Fryer and set the time for 8 minutes per side.
9. After cooking time is completed, remove the chicken strips from Air Fryer and serve hot.

Crispy Chicken Legs

Prep time: 15 minutes | Cook time: 20 minutes |Serves 6

- 480ml milk
- 250g flour
- 2 teaspoons garlic powder
- 2 teaspoons onion powder
- 2 teaspoons ground cumin
- 2 teaspoons paprika
- Salt and ground black pepper, as required
- 6 (200g) chicken legs

1. In a shallow bowl, place the milk.
2. In another shallow bowl, mix together the flour and spices.
3. Dip the chicken legs into milk and then coat with the flour mixture.
4. Repeat this process once again.
5. Grease basket of Ninja Foodi 2-Basket Air Fryer.
6. Press your chosen zone - "Zone 1" or "Zone 2" and then rotate the knob to select "Air Fry".
7. Set the temperature to 180 degrees C and then set the time for 5 minutes to preheat.
8. After preheating, arrange chicken legs in the basket of each zone.
9. Slide the basket into the Air Fryer and set the time for 25 minutes.
10. After cooking time is completed, remove the chicken legs from Air Fryer and serve hot.

Parmesan Chicken Breasts

Prep time: 15 minutes | Cook time: 22 minutes |Serves 4

- 4 (150g) chicken breasts
- 2 eggs, beaten
- 200g breadcrumbs
- 2 tablespoons fresh basil
- 4 tablespoons olive oil
- 120g pasta sauce
- 50g Parmesan cheese, grated

1. In a shallow bowl, beat the egg.
2. In another bowl, add the oil, breadcrumbs, and basil and mix until a crumbly mixture forms.
3. Now, dip each chicken breast into the beaten egg and then coat with the breadcrumb mixture.
4. Grease basket of Ninja Foodi 2-Basket Air Fryer.
5. Press your chosen zone - "Zone 1" or "Zone 2" and then rotate the knob to select "Air Fry".
6. Set the temperature to 175 degrees C and then set the time for 5 minutes to preheat.
7. After preheating, arrange 2 chicken breasts into the basket of each zone.
8. Slide the basket into the Air Fryer and set the time for 22 minutes.
9. After 15 minutes of cooking, spoon the pasta sauce over each chicken breast, followed by the cheese.
10. After cooking time is completed, remove the chicken breasts from Air Fryer and serve hot.

Rosemary Turkey Legs

Prep time: 10 minutes | Cook time: 30 minutes |Serves 4

- 4 garlic cloves, minced
- 2 tablespoons fresh rosemary, minced
- 2 teaspoons fresh lime zest, finely grated
- 4 tablespoons olive oil
- 2 tablespoons fresh lime juice
- Salt and ground black pepper, as required
- 4 turkey legs

1. In a large baking dish, mix together the garlic, rosemary, lime zest, oil, lime juice, salt, and black pepper.
2. Add the turkey legs and generously coat with marinade.
3. Refrigerate to marinate for about 6-8 hours.
4. Grease basket of Ninja Foodi 2-Basket Air Fryer.
5. Press your chosen zone - "Zone 1" or "Zone 2" and then rotate the knob to select "Air Fry".
6. Set the temperature to 175 degrees C and then set the time for 5 minutes to preheat.
7. After preheating, arrange 2 turkey legs into the basket of each zone.
8. Slide the basket into the Air Fryer and set the time for 30 minutes.
9. While cooking, flip the turkey legs once halfway through.
10. After cooking time is completed, remove the turkey legs from Air Fryer and serve hot.

Garlicky Duck Legs

Prep time: 10 minutes | Cook time: 30 minutes |Serves 4

- 4 garlic cloves, minced
- 2 tablespoons fresh parsley, chopped
- 2 teaspoons five-spice powder
- Salt and ground black pepper, as required
- 4 duck legs

1. In a bowl, add the garlic, parsley, five-spice powder, salt and black pepper and mix until well combined.
2. Rub the duck legs with garlic mixture generously.
3. Grease basket of Ninja Foodi 2-Basket Air Fryer.
4. Press your chosen zone - "Zone 1" or "Zone 2" and then rotate the knob to select "Air Fry".
5. Set the temperature to 170 degrees C and then set the time for 5 minutes to preheat.
6. After preheating, arrange 2 duck legs into the basket of each zone.
7. Slide the basket into the Air Fryer and set the time for 30 minutes.
8. After cooking time is completed, remove the duck legs from Air Fryer and serve hot.

Chapter 5
Beef, Lamb, and Pork Recipes

Exotic Beef and Plum Dish

Prep time: 10 minutes | Cook time: 40 minutes | Serves 4

- 1½ pounds beef stew meat, cubed
- 3 tablespoons honey
- 2 tablespoons olive oil
- 9 ounces plums, pitted and halved
- 8 ounces beef stock
- 2 yellow onions, chopped
- 2 garlic cloves, minced
- Salt and black pepper to tastes
- 1 teaspoon turmeric powder
- 1 teaspoon ginger powder
- 1 teaspoon cinnamon powder

1. In a pan that fits your air fryer, heats up the oil over medium heat.
2. Add the beef, stir, and brown for 2 minutes.
3. Add the honey, onions, garlic, salt, pepper, turmeric, ginger, and cinnamon; toss, and cook for 2-3 minutes more.
4. Add the plums and the stock; toss again.
5. Place the pan in the Fryer and cook at 380 degrees for 30 minutes.
6. Divide everything into bowls and serve.

Beef and Grape Roast

Prep time: 10 minutes | Cook time: 40 minutes | Serves 4

- 1-pound beef roast meat, cubed
- 3 tablespoons olive oil
- Salt and black pepper to taste
- 1½ cups chicken stock
- ½ cup dry white wine
- 2 garlic cloves, minced
- 1 teaspoon thyme, chopped
- ½ red onion, chopped
- ½ pound red grapes

1. Heat up the oil in a pan that fits your air fryer over medium-high heat.
2. Add the beef, salt, and pepper, toss, and brown for 5 minutes.
3. Add the stock, wine, garlic, thyme, and onions; toss and cook for 5 minutes more.
4. Transfer the pan to your air fryer and cook at 390 degrees F for 25 minutes.
5. Add the grapes, toss gently, and cook everything for 5-6 minutes more.
6. Divide between plates and serve right away.

Peas and Beef Mix

Prep time: 10 minutes | Cook time: 25 minutes | Serves 4

- 2 beef steaks, cut into strips
- Salt and black pepper to taste
- 14 ounces of snow peas
- 2 tablespoons soy sauce
- 1 tablespoon olive oil

1. Put all of the ingredients into a pan that fits your air fryer; toss well.
2. Place the pan in the Fryer and cook at 390 degrees F for 25 minutes.
3. Divide everything between plates and serve.

Paprika Beef

Prep time: 10 minutes | Cook time: 26 minutes | Serves 6

- 1½ pounds beef fillet
- 3 teaspoons sweet Paprika
- 2 tablespoons olive oil
- 1 tablespoon tomato paste
- ½ cup beef stock
- 1 tablespoon Worcestershire sauce
- 1 red onion, roughly chopped
- Salt and black pepper to taste

1. In a bowl, mix the beef with all remaining ingredients; toss well.
2. Transfer the mixture to a pan that fits your air fryer and cook at 400 degrees F for 26 minutes, shaking the air fryer halfway.
3. Divide everything between plates and serve.

Oregano and Asparagus Pork

Prep time: 10 minutes | Cook time: 35 minutes | Serves 6

- 2 pounds pork loin, boneless and cubed
- ¾ cup beef stock
- 2 tablespoons olive oil
- 3 tablespoons tomato sauce
- 1 pound asparagus, trimmed and halved
- ½ tablespoon oregano, chopped
- Salt and pepper to taste

1. Take a pan and place it over medium heat, add oil and let it heat up
2. Add pork and brown for 5 minutes
3. Add remaining ingredients and toss well
4. Preheat your Instant Vortex Air Fryer to 380 degrees F
5. Transfer mix to cooking basket and cook for 30 minutes
6. Serve and enjoy!

Simple Beef Rib Eye

Prep time: 5 minutes | Cook time: 16 minutes | Serves 4

- 2 pounds rib-eye steak
- 1 tablespoon olive oil
- Salt to taste
- Pepper to taste

1. Preheat your Air Fryer to 350-degree F
2. Take olive oil and rub it on both sides of the steak
3. Season with salt and pepper
4. Place the steaks in your Air fryer
5. Cook for 8 minutes
6. Flip the steak and cook for 8 minutes more
7. Serve and enjoy!

Beef Schnitzel

Prep time: 10 minutes | Cook time: 12 minutes | Serves 3

- 1 thin beef schnitzel
- 1 egg, whisked
- 2 tablespoons vegetable oil
- 2-ounce breadcrumbs
- 1 whole lemon

1. Preheat your Air Fryer to 356-degree F
2. Add breadcrumbs and vegetable oil into a bowl
3. Mix them well
4. Continue to stir the mixture
5. Dip the schnitzel into the Egg
6. Dredge the coated schnitzel into the bread crumb and coat well
7. Transfer them into Air fryer cooking basket
8. Cook for 12 minutes
9. Serve with lemon
10. Serve and enjoy!

Garlic and Bacon Platter

Prep time: 10 minutes | Cook time: 30 minutes | Serves 4

- 4 potatoes, halved and peeled
- 6 garlic cloves, unpeeled and squashed
- 4 streaky cut rashers bacon
- 2 sprigs rosemary
- 1 tablespoon olive oil

1. Preheat your Air Fryer to 390-degree F
2. Add bacon, potatoes, rosemary, and garlic
3. Add oil and mix it well
4. Transfer the mix to a frying basket
5. Roast for 25-30 minutes
6. Serve and enjoy!

Beef and Tomato Balls

Prep time: 10 minutes | Cook time: 5 minutes | Serves 4

- ¾ pounds ground beef
- 3 tablespoons almond meal
- 1 tablespoon fresh parsley, chopped
- 1 whole egg
- ½ tablespoon fresh thyme leaves, chopped
- 1 small onion, chopped
- Salt and pepper to taste

1. Preheat your Air Fryer to 390-degree F
2. Chop onion and keep them aside
3. Add all the listed ingredients into a bowl
4. Mix them well
5. Make 12 balls
6. Transfer balls to the Fryer
7. Cook for 8 minutes and transfer the balls to the oven
8. Add tomatoes sauce and drown the balls
9. Transfer the dish to your Air Fryer
10. Cook for 5 minutes at 300 degrees F
11. Stir occasionally
12. Serve and enjoy!

Mango Pork Fillet

Prep time: 10 minutes | Cook time: 12 minutes | Serves 6

- Calories 179
- Carbohydrates 11g
- Fat 13g
- Sugars 6g

1. Cut six pork medallions the same size as the pork loin you own.
2. Salt and pepper to your liking.
3. Use a cooking tool to spray a very small amount of olive oil.
4. Place your pork medallions on the air fryer previously preheated at 1500C and cook for 12 minutes.

Honey-Glazed Salmon

Prep time: 5 minutes | Cook time: 12 minutes | Serves 4

- 60 ml raw honey
- 4 garlic cloves, minced
- 1 tablespoon olive oil
- ½ teaspoon salt
- Olive oil cooking spray
- 4 (1½-inch-thick) salmon fillets

1. In a small bowl, mix together the honey, garlic, olive oil, and salt.
2. Spray the bottom and side of the zone 1 air fryer drawer with olive oil cooking spray, and place the salmon in a single layer in the zone 1 air fryer drawer.
3. Brush the top of each fillet with the honey-garlic mixture, and roast at 190°C for 10 to 12 minutes, or until the internal temperature reaches 64°C.

Baked Grouper with Tomatoes and Garlic

Prep time: 5 minutes | Cook time: 12 minutes | Serves 4

- 4 grouper fillets
- ½ teaspoon salt
- 3 garlic cloves, minced
- 1 tomato, sliced
- 45 g sliced Kalamata olives
- 10 g fresh dill, roughly chopped
- Juice of 1 lemon
- ¼ cup olive oil

1. Season the grouper fillets on all sides with salt, then place into the zone 1 air fryer drawer and top with the minced garlic, tomato slices, olives, and fresh dill.
2. Drizzle the lemon juice and olive oil over the top of the grouper, then bake at 190°C for 10 to 12 minutes, or until the internal temperature reaches 64°C.

Fried Catfish Fillets

Prep time: 10 minutes | Cook time: 20 minutes | Serves 4

- 1 egg
- 100 g finely ground cornmeal
- 30 g plain flour
- ¾ teaspoon salt
- 1 teaspoon paprika
- 1 teaspoon Old Bay seasoning
- ¼ teaspoon garlic powder
- ¼ teaspoon freshly ground black pepper
- 4 (140 g) catfish fillets, halved crosswise
- Olive oil spray

1. In a shallow bowl, beat the egg with 2 tablespoons water.
2. On a plate, stir together the cornmeal, flour, salt, paprika, Old Bay, garlic powder, and pepper.

3. Dip the fish into the egg mixture and into the cornmeal mixture to coat.
4. Press the cornmeal mixture into the fish and gently shake off any excess.
5. Place two baking paper liners into the two air fryer drawers.
6. Place the coated fish in half on the two liners and spray it with olive oil.
7. Air fry for 10 minutes, remove the drawers and spray the fish with olive oil.
8. Flip the fish and spray the other side with olive oil.
9. Reinsert the drawer to resume cooking.
10. Check the fish after 7 minutes more.
11. If the fish is golden and crispy and registers at least 64°C on a food thermometer, it is ready.
12. If not, resume cooking.
13. When the cooking is complete, serve.

Steamed Tuna with Lemongrass

Prep time: 10 minutes | Cook time: 10 minutes | Serves 4

- 4 small tuna steaks
- 2 tablespoons low-sodium soy sauce
- 2 teaspoons sesame oil
- 2 teaspoons rice wine vinegar
- 1 teaspoon grated peeled fresh ginger
- ⅛ teaspoon freshly ground black pepper
- 1 stalk lemongrass, bent in half
- 3 tablespoons freshly squeezed lemon juice

1. Place the tuna steaks on a plate.
2. In a small bowl, whisk the soy sauce, sesame oil, vinegar, and ginger until combined.
3. Pour this mixture over the tuna and gently rub it into both sides.
4. Sprinkle the fish with the pepper.
5. Let marinate for 10 minutes.
6. Place the lemongrass into the zone 1 drawer and top it with the tuna steaks.
7. Drizzle the tuna with the lemon juice and 1 tablespoon of water.
8. Roast at 200°C for 10 minutes.
9. When the cooking is complete, a food thermometer inserted into the tuna should register at least 64°C.
10. Discard the lemongrass and serve the tuna.

Tuna Steak

Prep time: 10 minutes | Cook time: 12 minutes | Serves 4

- 455 g tuna steaks, boneless and cubed
- 1 tablespoon mustard
- 1 tablespoon avocado oil
- 1 tablespoon apple cider vinegar

1. Mix avocado oil with mustard and apple cider vinegar.
2. Then brush tuna steaks with mustard mixture and put in half into the two air fryer drawers.
3. Air fry the fish at 182°C for 6 minutes per side.

Sesame-Crusted Tuna Steak

Prep time: 5 minutes | Cook time: 8 minutes | Serves 2

- 2 (170 g) tuna steaks
- 1 tablespoon coconut oil, melted
- ½ teaspoon garlic powder
- 2 teaspoons white sesame seeds
- 2 teaspoons black sesame seeds

1. Brush each tuna steak with coconut oil and sprinkle with garlic powder.
2. In a large bowl, mix sesame seeds and then press each tuna steak into them, covering the steak as completely as possible.
3. Place tuna steaks into the zone 1 air fryer drawer.
4. Adjust the temperature to 204°C and air fry for 8 minutes.
5. Flip the steaks halfway through the cooking time.
6. Steaks will be well-done at 64°C internal temperature.
7. Serve warm.

Simple Buttery Cod

Prep time: 5 minutes | Cook time: 8 minutes | Serves 2

- 2 x 110 g cod fillets
- 2 tablespoons salted butter, melted
- 1 teaspoon Old Bay seasoning
- ½ medium lemon, sliced

1. Place cod fillets into a round baking dish.
2. Brush each fillet with butter and sprinkle with Old Bay seasoning.
3. Lay two lemon slices on each fillet.
4. Cover the dish with foil and place into the zone 1 air fryer drawer.
5. Adjust the temperature to 176°C and bake for 8 minutes.
6. Flip halfway through the cooking time.
7. When cooked, internal temperature should be at least 64°C.
8. Serve warm.

Cod with Jalapeño

Prep time: 5 minutes | Cook time: 14 minutes | Serves 4

- 4 cod fillets, boneless
- 1 jalapeño, minced
- 1 tablespoon avocado oil
- ½ teaspoon minced garlic

1. In the shallow bowl, mix minced jalapeño, avocado oil, and minced garlic.
2. Put the cod fillets halves into the two air fryer drawers in one layer and top with minced jalapeño mixture.
3. Air fry the fish at 185°C for 7 minutes per side.

Scallops in Lemon-Butter Sauce

Prep time: 10 minutes | Cook time: 6 minutes | Serves 2

- 8 large dry sea scallops (about 340 g)
- Salt and freshly ground black pepper, to taste
- 2 tablespoons olive oil
- 2 tablespoons unsalted butter, melted
- 2 tablespoons chopped flat-leaf parsley
- 1 tablespoon fresh lemon juice
- 2 teaspoons capers, drained and chopped
- 1 teaspoon grated lemon zest
- 1 clove garlic, minced

1. Use a paper towel to pat the scallops dry.
2. Sprinkle lightly with salt and pepper.
3. Brush with the olive oil.
4. Arrange the scallops in a single layer halves into the two air fryer drawers.
5. Pausing halfway through the cooking time to turn the scallops, air fry at 200°C for about 6 minutes until firm and opaque.
6. Meanwhile, in a small bowl, combine the oil, butter, parsley, lemon juice, capers, lemon zest, and garlic.
7. Drizzle over the scallops just before serving.

Bacon-Wrapped Scallops

Prep time: 5 minutes | Cook time: 10 minutes | Serves 4

- 8 sea scallops, 30 g each, cleaned and patted dry
- 8 slices bacon
- ¼ teaspoon salt
- ¼ teaspoon ground black pepper

1. Wrap each scallop in 1 slice bacon and secure with a toothpick.
2. Sprinkle with salt and pepper.
3. Place scallops into the zone 1 ungreased air fryer drawer.
4. Adjust the temperature to 180°C and air fry for 10 minutes.
5. Scallops will be opaque and firm, and have an internal temperature of 56°C when done.
6. Serve warm.

Fried Prawns

Prep time: 15 minutes | Cook time: 5 minutes | Serves 4

- 70 g self-raising flour
- 1 teaspoon paprika
- 1 teaspoon salt
- ½ teaspoon freshly ground black pepper
- 1 large egg, beaten
- 120 g finely crushed panko bread crumbs
- 20 frozen large prawns (about 900 g), peeled and deveined
- Cooking spray

1. In a shallow bowl, whisk the flour, paprika, salt, and pepper until blended.
2. Add the beaten egg to a second shallow bowl and the bread crumbs to a third.
3. One at a time, dip the prawns into the flour, the egg, and the bread crumbs, coating thoroughly.
4. Line the two air fryer drawers with two baking papers.
5. Place the prawns on the two baking papers and spritz with oil.
6. Air fry at 200°C for 2 minutes.
7. Shake the drawer, spritz the prawns with oil, and air fry for 3 minutes more until lightly browned and crispy.
8. Serve hot.

Blackened Fish

Prep time: 15 minutes | Cook time: 8 minutes | Serves 4

- 1 large egg, beaten
- Blackened seasoning, as needed
- 2 tablespoons light brown sugar
- 4 x 110 g tilapia fillets
- Cooking spray

1. In a shallow bowl, place the beaten egg.
2. In a second shallow bowl, stir together the Blackened seasoning and the brown sugar.
3. One at a time, dip the fish fillets in the egg, then the brown sugar mixture, coating thoroughly.
4. Line the two air fryer drawers with two baking papers.
5. Place the coated fish on the baking papers and spritz with oil.
6. Bake at 150°C for 4 minutes.
7. Flip the fish, spritz it with oil, and bake for 4 to 6 minutes more until the fish is white inside and flakes easily with a fork.
8. Serve immediately.

Oyster Po'Boy

Prep time: 20 minutes | Cook time: 5 minutes | Serves 4

- 105 g plain flour
- 40 g yellow cornmeal
- 1 tablespoon Cajun seasoning
- 1 teaspoon salt
- 2 large eggs, beaten
- 1 teaspoon hot sauce
- 455 g pre-shucked oysters
- 1 (12-inch) French baguette, quartered and sliced horizontally
- Tartar Sauce, as needed
- 150 g shredded lettuce, divided
- 2 tomatoes, cut into slices
- Cooking spray

1. In a shallow bowl, whisk the flour, cornmeal, Cajun seasoning, and salt until blended.
2. In a second shallow bowl, whisk together the eggs and hot sauce.
3. One at a time, dip the oysters in the cornmeal mixture, the eggs, and again in the cornmeal, coating thoroughly.
4. Line the two air fryer drawers with two baking papers.
5. Place the oysters in half into the two drawers and spritz with oil.
6. Air fry at 200°C for 2 minutes.
7. Shake the drawers, spritz the oysters with oil, and air fry for 3 minutes more until lightly browned and crispy.
8. Spread each sandwich half with Tartar Sauce.
9. Assemble the po'boys by layering each sandwich with fried oysters, ½ cup shredded lettuce, and 2 tomato slices.
10. Serve immediately.

Trout Amandine with Lemon Butter Sauce

Prep time: 20 minutes | Cook time:8 minutes | Serves 4

- Trout Amandine:
- 65 g toasted almonds
- 30 g grated Parmesan cheese
- 1 teaspoon salt
- ½ teaspoon freshly ground black pepper
- 2 tablespoons butter, melted
- 4 x 110 g trout fillets, or salmon fillets
- Cooking spray
- Lemon Butter Sauce:
- 8 tablespoons butter, melted
- 2 tablespoons freshly squeezed lemon juice
- ½ teaspoon Worcestershire sauce
- ½ teaspoon salt
- ½ teaspoon freshly ground black pepper
- ¼ teaspoon hot sauce

1. In a blender or food processor, pulse the almonds for 5 to 10 seconds until finely processed.
2. Transfer to a shallow bowl and whisk in the Parmesan cheese, salt, and pepper.
3. Place the melted butter in another shallow bowl.
4. One at a time, dip the fish in the melted butter, then the almond mixture, coating thoroughly.
5. Line the two air fryer drawers with two baking papers.
6. Place the coated fish evenly on the baking papers of the two baking drawers and spritz with oil.
7. Bake at 150°C for 4 minutes. Flip the fish, spritz it with oil, and bake for 4 minutes more until the fish flakes easily with a fork.
8. In a small bowl, whisk the butter, lemon juice, Worcestershire sauce, salt, pepper, and hot sauce until blended.
9. Serve with the fish.

Fried Catfish with Dijon Sauce

Prep time: 20 minutes | Cook time: 7 minutes | Serves 4

- 4 tablespoons butter, melted
- 2 teaspoons Worcestershire sauce, divided
- 1 teaspoon lemon pepper
- 120 g panko bread crumbs
- 4 x 110 g catfish fillets
- Cooking spray
- 120 ml sour cream
- 1 tablespoon Dijon mustard

1. In a shallow bowl, stir together the melted butter, 1 teaspoon of Worcestershire sauce, and the lemon pepper.
2. Place the bread crumbs in another shallow bowl.
3. One at a time, dip both sides of the fillets in the butter mixture, then the bread crumbs, coating thoroughly.
4. Line the two air fryer drawers with two baking papers.
5. Place the coated fish on the baking papers and spritz with oil. Bake at 150°C for 4 minutes.
6. Flip the fish, spritz it with oil, and bake for 3 to 6 minutes more, depending on the thickness of the fillets, until the fish flakes easily with a fork.
7. In a small bowl, stir together the sour cream, Dijon, and remaining 1 teaspoon of Worcestershire sauce.
8. This sauce can be made 1 day in advance and refrigerated before serving.
9. Serve with the fried fish.

New Orleans-Style Crab Cakes

Prep time: 10 minutes | Cook time: 8 to 10 minutes | Serves 4

- 190 g bread crumbs
- 2 teaspoons Creole Seasoning
- 1 teaspoon dry mustard
- 1 teaspoon salt
- 1 teaspoon freshly ground black pepper
- 360 g crab meat
- 2 large eggs, beaten
- 1 teaspoon butter, melted
- ⅓ cup minced onion
- Cooking spray
- Tartar Sauce, for serving

1. Line the two air fryer drawers with baking papers.
2. In a medium bowl, whisk the bread crumbs, Creole Seasoning, dry mustard, salt, and pepper until blended.
3. Add the crab meat, eggs, butter, and onion. Stir until blended.
4. Shape the crab mixture into 8 patties.
5. Place the crab cakes in half on the baking papers in the two drawers and spritz with oil.
6. Air fry at 180°C for 4 minutes.
7. Flip the cakes, spritz them with oil, and air fry for 4 to 6 minutes more until the outsides are firm and a fork inserted into the center comes out clean.
8. Serve with the Tartar Sauce.

Mediterranean-Style Cod

Prep time: 5 minutes | Cook time: 12 minutes | Serves 4

- 4 cod fillets, 170 g each
- 3 tablespoons fresh lemon juice
- 1 tablespoon olive oil
- ¼ teaspoon salt
- 6 cherry tomatoes, halved
- 45 g pitted and sliced kalamata olives

1. Place cod into an ungreased round nonstick baking dish.
2. Pour lemon juice into dish and drizzle cod with olive oil.
3. Sprinkle with salt.
4. Place tomatoes and olives around baking dish in between fillets.
5. Place dish into the zone 1 air fryer drawer.
6. Bake at 180°C for 12 minutes, carefully turning cod halfway through cooking.
7. Fillets will be lightly browned, easily flake, and have an internal temperature of at least 64°C when done.
8. Serve warm.

Fish Sandwich with Tartar Sauce

Prep time: 10 minutes | Cook time: 17 minutes | Serves 2

- Tartar Sauce:
- 115 g mayonnaise
- 2 tablespoons onion granules
- 1 dill pickle spear, finely chopped
- 2 teaspoons pickle juice
- ¼ teaspoon salt
- ⅛ teaspoon ground black pepper
- Fish:
- 2 tablespoons plain flour
- 1 egg, lightly beaten
- 120 g panko
- 2 teaspoons lemon pepper
- 2 tilapia fillets
- Cooking spray
- 2 soft sub rolls

1. In a small bowl, combine the mayonnaise, onion granules, pickle, pickle juice, salt, and pepper.
2. Whisk to combine and chill in the refrigerator while you make the fish.
3. Place a baking paper liner in the zone 1 air fryer drawer.
4. Scoop the flour out onto a plate; set aside.
5. Put the beaten egg in a medium shallow bowl.
6. On another plate, mix to combine the panko and lemon pepper.
7. Dredge the tilapia fillets in the flour, then dip in the egg, and then press into the panko mixture.
8. Place the prepared fillets on the liner in the zone 1 air fryer drawer in a single layer.
9. Spray lightly with cooking spray and air fry at 200°C for 8 minutes.
10. Carefully flip the fillets, spray with more cooking spray, and air fry for an additional 9 minutes, until golden and crispy.

Lemony Prawns and Courgette

Prep time: 15 minutes | Cook time: 7 to 8 minutes | Serves 4

- 570 g extra-large raw prawns, peeled and deveined
- 2 medium courgettes (about 230 g each), halved lengthwise and cut into ½-inch-thick slices
- 1½ tablespoons olive oil
- ½ teaspoon garlic salt
- 1½ teaspoons dried oregano
- ⅛ teaspoon crushed red pepper flakes (optional)
- Juice of ½ lemon
- 1 tablespoon chopped fresh mint
- 1 tablespoon chopped fresh dill

1. In a large bowl, combine the prawns, courgette, oil, garlic salt, oregano, and pepper flakes (if using) and toss to coat.
2. Arrange a single layer of the prawns and courgette in the two air fryer drawers.
3. You may need to work in batches.
4. Air fry at 180°C for 7 to 8 minutes, shaking the drawer halfway, until the courgette is golden and the prawns are cooked through.
5. Transfer to a serving dish and tent with foil.
6. Top with the lemon juice, mint, and dill and serve.

Roasted Fish with Almond-Lemon Crumbs

Prep time: 10 minutes | Cook time: 7 to 8 minutes | Serves 4

- 70 g raw whole almonds
- 1 spring onion, finely chopped
- Grated zest and juice of 1 lemon
- ½ tablespoon extra-virgin olive oil
- ¾ teaspoon kosher or coarse sea salt, divided
- Freshly ground black pepper, to taste
- 4 (170 g) skinless fish fillets
- Cooking spray
- 1 teaspoon Dijon mustard

1. In a food processor, pulse the almonds to coarsely chop.
2. Transfer to a small bowl and add the scallion, lemon zest, and olive oil.
3. Season with ¼ teaspoon of the salt and pepper to taste and mix to combine.
4. Spray the top of the fish with oil and squeeze the lemon juice over the fish.
5. Season with the remaining ½ teaspoon salt and pepper to taste.
6. Spread the mustard on top of the fish.
7. Place the fillets in the two air fryer drawers in a single layer.
8. Air fry at 192°C for 7 to 8 minutes, until the crumbs start to brown and the fish is cooked through.
9. Serve immediately.

Chickpea Fritters

Prep time: 10 minutes | Cook time: 6 minutes | Serves 6

- 237ml plain yogurt
- 2 tablespoons sugar
- 1 tablespoon honey
- ½ teaspoon salt
- ½ teaspoon black pepper
- ½ teaspoon crushed red pepper flakes
- 1 can (28g) chickpeas, drained
- 1 teaspoon ground cumin
- ½ teaspoon salt
- ½ teaspoon garlic powder
- ½ teaspoon ground ginger
- 1 large egg
- ½ teaspoon baking soda
- ½ cup fresh coriander, chopped
- 2 green onions, sliced

1. Mash chickpeas with rest of the ingredients in a food processor.
2. Layer the two air fryer baskets with a parchment paper.
3. Drop the batter in the baskets spoon by spoon.
4. Return the air fryer basket 1 to Zone 1, and basket 2 to Zone 2 of the Ninja Foodi 2-Basket Air Fryer.
5. Choose the "Air Fry" mode for Zone 1 at 400 degrees F and 6 minutes of cooking time.
6. Select the "MATCH COOK" option to copy the settings for Zone 2.
7. Initiate cooking by pressing the START/PAUSE BUTTON.
8. Flip the fritters once cooked halfway through.
9. Serve warm.

Mushroom Roll-Ups

Prep time: 15 minutes | Cook time: 11 minutes | Serves 10

- 2 tablespoons olive oil
- 227g portobello mushrooms, chopped
- 1 teaspoon dried oregano
- 1 teaspoon dried thyme
- ½ teaspoon crushed red pepper flakes
- ¼ teaspoon salt
- 1 package (227g) cream cheese, softened
- 113g whole-milk ricotta cheese
- 10 (8 inches) flour tortillas
- Cooking spray
- Chutney

1. Sauté mushrooms with oil, thyme, salt, pepper flakes, and oregano in a skillet for 4 minutes.
2. Mix cheeses and add sauteed mushrooms the mix well.
3. Divide the mushroom mixture over the tortillas.
4. Roll the tortillas and secure with a toothpick.
5. Place the rolls in the air fryer basket.
6. Return the air fryer basket 1 to Zone 1, and basket 2 to Zone 2 of the Ninja Foodi 2-Basket Air Fryer.
7. Choose the "Air Fry" mode for Zone 1 and set the temperature to 400 degrees F and 11 minutes of cooking time.
8. Select the "MATCH COOK" option to copy the settings for Zone 2.
9. Initiate cooking by pressing the START/PAUSE BUTTON.
10. Flip the rolls once cooked halfway through.
11. Serve warm.

Potatoes & Beans

Prep time: 10 minutes | Cook time: 25 minutes | Serves 4

- 453g potatoes, cut into pieces
- 15ml olive oil
- 1 tsp garlic powder
- 160g green beans, trimmed
- Pepper
- Salt

1. In a bowl, toss green beans, garlic powder, potatoes, oil, pepper, and salt.
2. Insert a crisper plate in the Ninja Foodi air fryer baskets.
3. Add green beans and potato mixture to both baskets.
4. Select zone 1 then select "air fry" mode and set the temperature to 380 degrees F for 25 minutes. Press "match" to match zone 2 settings to zone 1. Press "start/stop" to begin. Stir halfway through.

Bacon Potato Patties

Prep time: 10 minutes | Cook time: 15 minutes | Serves 2

- 1 egg
- 600g mashed potatoes
- 119g breadcrumbs
- 2 bacon slices, cooked & chopped
- 235g cheddar cheese, shredded
- 15g flour
- Pepper
- Salt

1. In a bowl, mix mashed potatoes with remaining ingredients until well combined.
2. Make patties from potato mixture and place on a plate.
3. Place plate in the refrigerator for 10 minutes
4. Insert a crisper plate in the Ninja Foodi air fryer baskets.
5. Place the prepared patties in both baskets.
6. Select zone 1 then select "air fry" mode and set the temperature to 390 degrees F for 15 minutes. Press "match" to match zone 2 settings to zone 1. Press "start/stop" to begin. Turn halfway through.

Herb and Lemon Cauliflower

Prep time: 10 minutes | Cook time: 10 minutes | Serves 4

- 1 cauliflower head, cut into florets
- 4 tablespoons olive oil
- ¼ cup fresh parsley
- 1 tablespoon fresh rosemary
- 1 tablespoon fresh thyme
- 1 teaspoon lemon zest, grated
- 2 tablespoons lemon juice
- ½ teaspoon salt
- ¼ teaspoon crushed red pepper flakes

1. Toss cauliflower with oil, herbs and the rest of the ingredients in a bowl.
2. Divide the seasoned cauliflower in the air fryer baskets.
3. Return the air fryer basket 1 to Zone 1, and basket 2 to Zone 2 of the Ninja Foodi 2-Basket Air Fryer.
4. Choose the "Air Fry" mode for Zone 1 at 350 degrees F and 10 minutes of cooking time.
5. Select the "MATCH COOK" option to copy the settings for Zone 2.
6. Initiate cooking by pressing the START/PAUSE BUTTON.
7. Serve warm.

Acorn Squash Slices

Prep time: 15 minutes | Cook time: 10 minutes | Serves 6

- 2 medium acorn squashes
- ⅔ cup packed brown sugar
- ½ cup butter, melted

1. Cut the squash in half, remove the seeds and slice into ½ inch slices.
2. Place the squash slices in the air fryer baskets.
3. Drizzle brown sugar and butter over the squash slices.
4. Return the air fryer basket 1 to Zone 1, and basket 2 to Zone 2 of the Ninja Foodi 2-Basket Air Fryer.
5. Choose the "Air Fry" mode for Zone 1 and set the temperature to 350 degrees F and 10 minutes of cooking time.
6. Select the "MATCH COOK" option to copy the settings for Zone 2.
7. Initiate cooking by pressing the START/PAUSE BUTTON.
8. Flip the squash once cooked halfway through.
9. Serve.

Green Tomato Stacks

Prep time: 15 minutes | Cook time: 12 minutes | Serves 6

- ¼ cup mayonnaise
- ¼ teaspoon lime zest, grated
- 2 tablespoons lime juice
- 1 teaspoon minced fresh thyme
- ½ teaspoon black pepper
- ¼ cup all-purpose flour
- 2 large egg whites, beaten
- ¾ cup cornmeal
- ¼ teaspoon salt
- 2 medium green tomatoes
- 2 medium re tomatoes
- Cooking spray
- 8 slices Canadian bacon, warmed

1. Mix mayonnaise with ¼ teaspoon black pepper, thyme, lime juice and zest in a bowl.
2. Spread flour in one bowl, beat egg whites in another bowl and mix cornmeal with ¼ teaspoon black pepper and salt in a third bowl.
3. Cut the tomatoes into 4 slices and coat each with the flour then dip in the egg whites.
4. Coat the tomatoes slices with the cornmeal mixture.
5. Place the slices in the air fryer baskets.
6. Return the air fryer basket 1 to Zone 1, and basket 2 to Zone 2 of the Ninja Foodi 2-Basket Air Fryer.
7. Choose the "Air Fry" mode for Zone 1 at 390 degrees F and 12 minutes of cooking time.
8. Select the "MATCH COOK" option to copy the settings for Zone 2.
9. Initiate cooking by pressing the START/PAUSE BUTTON.
10. Flip the tomatoes once cooked halfway through.
11. Place the green tomato slices on the working surface.
12. Top them with bacon, and red tomato slice.
13. Serve.

Healthy Air Fried Veggies

Prep time: 10 minutes | Cook time: 15 minutes | Serves 4

- 52g onion, sliced
- 71g broccoli florets
- 116g radishes, sliced
- 15ml olive oil
- 100g Brussels sprouts, cut in half
- 325g cauliflower florets
- 1 tsp balsamic vinegar
- ½ tsp garlic powder
- Pepper
- Salt

1. In a bowl, toss veggies with oil, vinegar, garlic powder, pepper, and salt.
2. Insert a crisper plate in the Ninja Foodi air fryer baskets.
3. Add veggies in both baskets.
4. Select zone 1 then select "air fry" mode and set the temperature to 380 degrees F for 15 minutes. Press "match" to match zone 2 settings to zone 1. Press "start/stop" to begin. Stir halfway through.

Air-Fried Radishes

Prep time: 10 minutes | Cook time: 15 minutes | Serves 6

- 1020g radishes, quartered
- 3 tablespoons olive oil
- 1 tablespoon fresh oregano, minced
- ¼ teaspoon salt
- ⅛ teaspoon black pepper

1. Toss radishes with oil, black pepper, salt and oregano in a bowl.
2. Divide the radishes into the Ninja Foodi 2 Baskets Air Fryer baskets.
3. Return the air fryer basket 1 to Zone 1, and basket 2 to Zone 2 of the Ninja Foodi 2-Basket Air Fryer.
4. Choose the "Air Fry" mode for Zone 1 at 375 degrees F and 15 minutes of cooking time.
5. Select the "MATCH COOK" option to copy the settings for Zone 2.
6. Initiate cooking by pressing the START/PAUSE BUTTON.
7. Toss the radishes once cooked halfway through.
8. Serve.

Fried Patty Pan Squash

Prep time: 10 minutes | Cook time: 15 minutes | Serves 6

- 5 cups small pattypan squash, halved
- 1 tablespoon olive oil
- 2 garlic cloves, minced
- ½ teaspoon salt
- ¼ teaspoon dried oregano
- ¼ teaspoon dried thyme
- ¼ teaspoon pepper
- 1 tablespoon minced parsley

1. Rub the squash with oil, garlic and the rest of the ingredients.
2. Spread the squash in the air fryer baskets.
3. Return the air fryer basket 1 to Zone 1, and basket 2 to Zone 2 of the Ninja Foodi 2-Basket Air Fryer.
4. Choose the "Air Fry" mode for Zone 1 at 375 degrees F and 15 minutes of cooking time.
5. Select the "MATCH COOK" option to copy the settings for Zone 2.
6. Initiate cooking by pressing the START/PAUSE BUTTON.
7. Flip the squash once cooked halfway through.
8. Garnish with parsley.
9. Serve warm.

Bacon Wrapped Corn Cob

Prep time: 15 minutes | Cook time: 10 minutes | Serves 4

- 4 trimmed corns on the cob
- 8 bacon slices

1. Wrap the corn cobs with two bacon slices.
2. Place the wrapped cobs into the Ninja Foodi 2 Baskets Air Fryer baskets.
3. Return the air fryer basket 1 to Zone 1, and basket 2 to Zone 2 of the Ninja Foodi 2-Basket Air Fryer.
4. Choose the "Air Fry" mode for Zone 1 and set the temperature to 355 degrees F and 10 minutes of cooking time.
5. Select the "MATCH COOK" option to copy the settings for Zone 2.
6. Initiate cooking by pressing the START/PAUSE BUTTON.
7. Flip the corn cob once cooked halfway through.
8. Serve warm.

Breaded Summer Squash

Prep time: 15 minutes | Cook time: 10 minutes | Serves 4

- 4 cups yellow summer squash, sliced
- 3 tablespoons olive oil
- ½ teaspoon salt
- ½ teaspoon pepper
- ⅛ teaspoon cayenne pepper
- ¾ cup panko bread crumbs
- ¾ cup grated Parmesan cheese

1. Mix crumbs, cheese, cayenne pepper, black pepper, salt and oil in a bowl.
2. Coat the squash slices with the breadcrumb mixture.
3. Place these slices in the air fryer baskets.
4. Return the air fryer basket 1 to Zone 1, and basket 2 to Zone 2 of the Ninja Foodi 2-Basket Air Fryer.
5. Choose the "Air Fry" mode for Zone 1 at 350 degrees F and 10 minutes of cooking time.
6. Select the "MATCH COOK" option to copy the settings for Zone 2.
7. Initiate cooking by pressing the START/PAUSE BUTTON.
8. Flip the squash slices once cooked half way through.
9. Serve warm.

Delicious Potatoes & Carrots

Prep time: 10 minutes | Cook time: 25 minutes | Serves 8

- 453g carrots, sliced
- 2 tsp smoked paprika
- 21g sugar
- 30ml olive oil
- 453g potatoes, diced
- ¼ tsp thyme
- ½ tsp dried oregano
- 1 tsp garlic powder
- Pepper
- Salt

1. In a bowl, toss carrots and potatoes with 1 tablespoon of oil.
2. Insert a crisper plate in the Ninja Foodi air fryer baskets.
3. Add carrots and potatoes to both baskets.
4. Select zone 1 then select "air fry" mode and set the temperature to 390 degrees F for 15 minutes. Press "match" to match zone 2 settings to zone 1. Press "start/stop" to begin.
5. In a mixing bowl, add cooked potatoes, carrots, smoked paprika, sugar, oil, thyme, oregano, garlic powder, pepper, and salt and toss well.
6. Return carrot and potato mixture into the air fryer basket and cook for 10 minutes more.

BBQ Corn

Prep time: 10 minutes | Cook time: 10 minutes | Serves 4

- 450g can baby corn, drained & rinsed
- 56g BBQ sauce
- ½ tsp Sriracha sauce

1. In a bowl, toss the baby corn with sriracha sauce and BBQ sauce until well coated.
2. Insert a crisper plate in the Ninja Foodi air fryer baskets.
3. Add the baby corn to both baskets.
4. Select zone 1, then select "air fry" mode and set the temperature to 390 degrees F for 10 minutes. Press "match" to match zone 2 settings to zone 1. Press "start/stop" to begin. Stir halfway through.

Lemon Herb Cauliflower

Prep time: 10 minutes | Cook time: 10 minutes | Serves 4

- 384g cauliflower florets
- 1 tsp lemon zest, grated
- 1 tbsp thyme, minced
- 60ml olive oil
- 1 tbsp rosemary, minced
- ¼ tsp red pepper flakes, crushed
- 30ml lemon juice
- 25g parsley, minced
- ½ tsp salt

1. In a bowl, toss cauliflower florets with the remaining ingredients until well coated.
2. Insert a crisper plate in the Ninja Foodi air fryer baskets.
3. Add cauliflower florets into both baskets.
4. Select zone 1, then select "air fry" mode and set the temperature to 360 degrees F for 10 minutes. Press "match" and "start/stop" to begin.

Broccoli, Squash, & Pepper

Prep time: 10 minutes | Cook time: 12 minutes | Serves 4

- 175g broccoli florets
- 1 red bell pepper, diced
- 1 tbsp olive oil
- ½ tsp garlic powder
- ¼ onion, sliced
- 1 zucchini, sliced
- 2 yellow squash, sliced
- Pepper
- Salt

1. In a bowl, toss veggies with oil, garlic powder, pepper, and salt.
2. Insert a crisper plate in the Ninja Foodi air fryer baskets.
3. Add the vegetable mixture in both baskets.
4. Select zone 1 then select "air fry" mode and set the temperature to 390 degrees F for 12 minutes. Press "match" to match zone 2 settings to zone 1. Press "start/stop" to begin. Stir halfway through.

Sweet Potatoes & Brussels Sprouts

Prep time: 10 minutes | Cook time: 35 minutes | Serves 8

- 340g sweet potatoes, cubed
- 30ml olive oil
- 150g onion, cut into pieces
- 352g Brussels sprouts, halved
- Pepper
- Salt
- 78ml ketchup
- 115ml balsamic vinegar
- 15g mustard
- 29 ml honey

1. In a bowl, toss Brussels sprouts, oil, onion, sweet potatoes, pepper, and salt.
2. Insert a crisper plate in the Ninja Foodi air fryer baskets.
3. Add Brussels sprouts and sweet potato mixture in both baskets.
4. Select zone 1, then select "air fry" mode and set the temperature to 390 degrees F for 25 minutes. Press "match" to match zone 2 settings to zone 1. Press "start/stop" to begin. Stir halfway through.
5. Meanwhile, add vinegar, ketchup, honey, and mustard to a saucepan and cook over medium heat for 5-10 minutes.
6. Toss cooked sweet potatoes and Brussels sprouts with sauce.

Rosemary Asparagus & Potatoes

Prep time: 10 minutes | Cook time: 30 minutes | Serves 6

- 125g asparagus, trimmed & cut into pieces
- 2 tsp garlic powder
- 2 tbsp rosemary, chopped
- 30ml olive oil
- 679g baby potatoes, quartered
- ½ tsp red pepper flakes
- Pepper
- Salt

1. Insert a crisper plate in the Ninja Foodi air fryer baskets.
2. Toss potatoes with 1 tablespoon of oil, pepper, and salt in a bowl until well coated.
3. Add potatoes into in zone 1 basket.
4. Toss asparagus with remaining oil, red pepper flakes, pepper, garlic powder, and rosemary in a mixing bowl.
5. Add asparagus into the zone 2 basket.
6. Select zone 1, then select "air fry" mode and set the temperature to 390 degrees F for 20 minutes. Select zone 2, then select "air fry" mode and set the temperature to 390 degrees F for 10 minutes. Press "match" mode, then press "start/stop" to begin.

Air Fryer Vegetables

Prep time: 15 minutes | Cook time: 15 minutes | Serves 2

- 1 courgette, diced
- 2 capsicums, diced
- 1 head broccoli, diced
- 1 red onion, diced
- 1 teaspoon smoked paprika
- 1 teaspoon garlic granules
- 1 teaspoon Herb de Provence
- Salt and black pepper, to taste
- 1½ tablespoon olive oil
- 2 tablespoons lemon juice

1. Toss the veggies with the rest of the marinade ingredients in a bowl.
2. Spread the veggies in the air fryer baskets.
3. Return the air fryer basket 1 to Zone 1, and basket 2 to Zone 2 of the Ninja Foodi 2-Basket Air Fryer.
4. Choose the "Air Fry" mode for Zone 1 at 400 degrees F and 15 minutes of cooking time.
5. Select the "MATCH COOK" option to copy the settings for Zone 2.
6. Initiate cooking by pressing the START/PAUSE BUTTON.
7. Toss the veggies once cooked half way through.
8. Serve warm.

Garlic-Rosemary Brussels Sprouts

Prep time: 15 minutes | Cook time: 8 minutes | Serves 4

- 3 tablespoons olive oil
- 2 garlic cloves, minced
- ½ teaspoon salt
- ¼ teaspoon black pepper
- 455g Brussels sprouts, halved
- ½ cup panko bread crumbs
- 1-½ teaspoons rosemary, minced

1. Toss the Brussels sprouts with crumbs and the rest of the ingredients in a bowl.
2. Divide the sprouts into the Ninja Foodi 2 Baskets Air Fryer baskets.
3. Return the air fryer basket 1 to Zone 1, and basket 2 to Zone 2 of the Ninja Foodi 2-Basket Air Fryer.
4. Choose the "Air Fry" mode for Zone 1 at 350 degrees F and 8 minutes of cooking time.
5. Select the "MATCH COOK" option to copy the settings for Zone 2.
6. Initiate cooking by pressing the START/PAUSE BUTTON.
7. Toss the Brussels sprouts once cooked halfway through.
8. Serve warm.

Balsamic Vegetables

Prep time: 10 minutes | Cook time: 13 minutes | Serves 4

- 125g asparagus, cut woody ends
- 88g mushrooms, halved
- 1 tbsp Dijon mustard
- 3 tbsp soy sauce
- 27g brown sugar
- 57ml balsamic vinegar
- 32g olive oil
- 1 zucchini, sliced
- 1 yellow squash, sliced
- 170g grape tomatoes
- Pepper
- Salt

1. In a bowl, mix asparagus, tomatoes, oil, mustard, soy sauce, mushrooms, zucchini, squash, brown sugar, vinegar, pepper, and salt.
2. Cover the bowl and place it in the refrigerator for 45 minutes.
3. Insert a crisper plate in the Ninja Foodi air fryer baskets.
4. Add the vegetable mixture in both baskets.
5. Select zone 1, then select "air fry" mode and set the temperature to 390 degrees F for 12 minutes. Press "match" to match zone 2 settings to zone 1. Press "start/stop" to begin. Stir halfway through.

Flavourful Mexican Cauliflower

Prep time: 10 minutes | Cook time: 12 minutes | Serves 4

- 1 medium cauliflower head, cut into florets
- ½ tsp turmeric
- 1 tsp onion powder
- 2 tsp garlic powder
- 2 tsp parsley
- 1 lime juice
- 30ml olive oil
- 1 tsp chilli powder
- 1 tsp cumin
- Pepper
- Salt

1. In a bowl, toss cauliflower florets with onion powder, garlic powder, parsley, oil, chilli powder, turmeric, cumin, pepper, and salt.
2. Insert a crisper plate in the Ninja Foodi air fryer baskets.
3. Add cauliflower florets in both baskets.
4. Select zone 1, then select "air fry" mode and set the temperature to 390 degrees F for 12 minutes. Press "match" to match zone 2 settings to zone 1. Press "start/stop" to begin. Stir halfway through.
5. Drizzle lime juice over cauliflower florets.

Chapter 8
Desserts Recipes

Bread Pudding

Prep time: 12 minutes | Cook time: 8-12 minutes | Serves 2

- Nonstick spray, for greasing ramekins
- 2 slices of white bread, crumbled
- 4 tablespoons white sugar
- 5 large eggs
- ½ cup cream
- Salt, pinch
- ⅓ teaspoon cinnamon powder

1. Take a bowl and whisk eggs in it.
2. Add sugar and salt to the eggs and whisk it all well.
3. Then add cream and use a hand beater to incorporate the ingredients.
4. Next add cinnamon, and the crumbled white bread.
5. Mix it well and add into two round shaped baking pans.
6. Place each baking pan in the air fryer basket.
7. Set zone 1 to AIR FRY mode at 350 degrees F/ 175 degrees C for 8-12 minutes.
8. Press MATCH button for zone 2.
9. Once it's cooked, serve.

Mini Strawberry and Cream Pies

Prep time: 12 minutes | Cook time: 10 minutes | Serves 2

- 1 box store-bought pie dough, Trader Joe's
- 1 cup strawberries, cubed
- 3 tablespoons cream, heavy
- 2 tablespoons almonds
- 1 egg white, for brushing

1. Take the store-bought pie dough and flatten it on a surface.
2. Use a round cutter to cut it into 3-inch circles.
3. Brush the dough with egg white all around the edges.
4. Now add almonds, strawberries, and cream in a tiny amount in the center of the dough, and top it with another dough circle.
5. Press the edges with a fork to seal it.
6. Make a slit in the middle of the pie and divide them into the baskets.
7. Set zone 1 to AIR FRY mode 360 degrees F/ 180 degrees C for 10 minutes.
8. Select MATCH for zone 2 basket.
9. Once done, serve.

Mini Blueberry Pies

Prep time: 12 minutes | Cook time: 10 minutes | Serves 2

- 1 box store-bought pie dough, Trader Joe's
- ¼ cup blueberry jam
- 1 teaspoon lemon zest
- 1 egg white, for brushing

1. Take the store-bought pie dough and cut it into 3-inch circles.
2. Brush the dough with egg white all around the edges.
3. Now add blueberry jam and zest in the middle and top it with another circle.
4. Press the edges with a fork to seal it.
5. Make a slit in the middle of each pie and divide them between the baskets.
6. Set zone 1 to AIR FRY mode 360 degrees F/ 180 degrees C for 10 minutes.
7. Select the MATCH button for zone 2.
8. Once cooked, serve.

Lemony Sweet Twists

Prep time: 15 minutes | Cook time: 9 minutes | Serves 2

- 1 box store-bought puff pastry
- ½ teaspoon lemon zest
- 1 tablespoon lemon juice
- 2 teaspoons brown sugar
- Salt, pinch
- 2 tablespoons Parmesan cheese, freshly grated

1. Put the puff pastry dough on a clean work surface.
2. In a bowl, combine Parmesan cheese, brown sugar, salt, lemon zest, and lemon juice.
3. Press this mixture into both sides of the dough.
4. Now, cut the pastry into 1" x 4" strips.
5. Twist 2 times from each end.
6. Place the strips into the air fryer baskets.
7. Select zone 1 to AIR FRY mode at 400 degrees F/ 200 degrees C for 9-10 minutes.
8. Select MATCH for zone 2 basket.
9. Once cooked, serve and enjoy.

Air Fryer Sweet Twists

Prep time: 15 minutes | Cook time: 9 minutes | Serves 2

- 1 box store-bought puff pastry
- ½ teaspoon cinnamon
- ½ teaspoon sugar
- ½ teaspoon black sesame seeds
- Salt, pinch
- 2 tablespoons Parmesan cheese, freshly grated

1. Place the dough on a work surface.
2. Take a small bowl and mix in cheese, sugar, salt, sesame seeds, and cinnamon.
3. Press this mixture on both sides of the dough.
4. Now, cut the pastry into 1" x 3" strips.
5. Twist each of the strips twice from each end.
6. Transfer them to both the air fryer baskets.
7. Select zone 1 to AIR FRY mode at 400 degrees F/ 200 degrees C for 9-10 minutes.
8. Select the MATCH button for the zone 2 basket.
9. Once cooked, serve.

Fudge Brownies

Prep time: 20 minutes | Cook time: 16 minutes | Serves 4

- ½ cup all-purpose flour
- ¼ cup unsweetened cocoa powder
- ¾ teaspoon kosher salt
- 2 large eggs, whisked
- 1 tablespoon almond milk
- ½ cup brown sugar
- ½ cup packed white sugar
- ½ tablespoon vanilla extract
- 8 ounces semisweet chocolate chips, melted
- ½ cup unsalted butter, melted

1. Take a medium bowl, and use a hand beater to whisk together eggs, milk, both the sugars and vanilla.
2. In a separate microwave-safe bowl, mix the melted butter and chocolate and microwave it for 30 seconds to melt the chocolate.
3. Add all the dry ingredients to the chocolate mixture.
4. Slowly add the egg mixture to the bowl.
5. Spray a reasonable round baking pan and pour the batter into the pan.
6. Select the AIR FRY mode and adjust the setting the temperature to 300 degrees F/ 150 degrees C, for 30 minutes.
7. Check it after 30 minutes and if not done, cook for 10 more minutes.
8. Once it's done, take it out and let it cool before serving.
9. Enjoy.

Churros

Prep time: 10 minutes | Cook time: 10 minutes | Serves 8

- 1 cup water
- ⅓ cup unsalted butter, cut into cubes
- 2 tablespoons granulated sugar
- ¼ teaspoon salt
- 1 cup all-purpose flour
- 2 large eggs
- 1 teaspoon vanilla extract
- Cooking oil spray
- ½ cup granulated sugar
- ¾ teaspoon ground cinnamon

1. Add the water, butter, sugar, and salt to a medium pot. Bring to a boil over medium-high heat.
2. Reduce the heat to medium-low and stir in the flour. Cook, stirring constantly with a rubber spatula until the dough is smooth and comes together.
3. Remove the dough from the heat and place it in a mixing bowl. Allow 4 minutes for cooling.
4. In a mixing bowl, beat the eggs and vanilla extract with an electric hand mixer or stand mixer until the dough comes together. The finished product will resemble gluey mashed potatoes. Press the lumps together into a ball with your hands, then transfer to a large piping bag with a large star-shaped tip. Pipe out the churros.
5. Install a crisper plate in both drawers. Place half the churros in the zone 1 drawer and half in zone 2's, then insert the drawers into the unit.
6. Select zone 1, select AIR FRY, set temperature to 390 degrees F/ 200 degrees C, and set time to 12 minutes. Select MATCH to match zone 2 settings to zone 1. Press the START/STOP button to begin cooking.
7. In a shallow bowl, combine the granulated sugar and cinnamon.
8. Immediately transfer the baked churros to the bowl with the sugar mixture and toss to coat.

Apple Fritters

Prep time: 10 minutes | Cook time: 10 minutes | Serves 4

- 2 large apples
- 2 cups all-purpose flour
- ½ cup granulated sugar
- 1 tablespoon baking powder
- 1 teaspoon salt
- 1 teaspoon ground cinnamon
- ½ teaspoon ground nutmeg
- ¼ teaspoon ground cloves
- ¾ cup apple cider or apple juice
- 2 eggs
- 3 tablespoons butter, melted
- 1 teaspoon vanilla extract
- 2 cups powdered sugar
- ¼ cup apple cider or apple juice
- ½ teaspoon ground cinnamon
- ¼ teaspoon ground nutmeg

1. Peel and core the apples, then cut them into ¼-inch cubes. Spread the apple chunks out on a kitchen towel to absorb any excess moisture.
2. In a mixing bowl, combine the flour, sugar, baking powder, salt, and spices.
3. Add the apple chunks and combine well.
4. Whisk together the apple cider, eggs, melted butter, and vanilla in a small bowl.
5. Combine the wet and dry ingredients in a large mixing bowl.
6. Install a crisper plate in both drawers. Use an ice cream scoop to scoop 3 to 4 dollops of fritter dough into the zone 1 drawer and 3 to 4 dollops into the zone 2 drawer. Insert the drawers into the unit. You may need to cook in batches.
7. Select zone 1, select BAKE, set temperature to 390 degrees F/ 200 degrees C, and set time to 10 minutes. Select MATCH to match zone 2 settings to zone 1. Press the START/STOP button to begin cooking.
8. Meanwhile, make the glaze: Whisk the powdered sugar, apple cider, and spices together until smooth.
9. When the fritters are cooked, drizzle the glaze over them. Let sit for 10 minutes until the glaze sets.

Pumpkin Muffins with Cinnamon

Prep time: 20 minutes | Cook time: 20 minutes | Serves 4

- 1 and ½ cups all-purpose flour
- ½ teaspoon baking soda
- ½ teaspoon baking powder
- 1 and ¼ teaspoons cinnamon, groaned
- ¼ teaspoon ground nutmeg, grated
- 2 large eggs
- Salt, pinch
- ¾ cup granulated sugar
- ½ cup dark brown sugar
- 1 and ½ cups pumpkin puree
- ¼ cup coconut milk

1. Take 4 ramekins and layer them with muffin paper.
2. In a bowl, add the eggs, brown sugar, baking soda, baking powder, cinnamon, nutmeg, and sugar and whisk well with an electric mixer.
3. In a second bowl, mix the flour, and salt.
4. Slowly add the dry ingredients to the wet ingredients.
5. Fold in the pumpkin puree and milk and mix it in well.
6. Divide this batter into 4 ramekins.
7. Place two ramekins in each air fryer basket.
8. Set the time for zone 1 to 18 minutes at 360 degrees F/ 180 degrees C on AIR FRY mode.
9. Select the MATCH button for the zone 2 basket.
10. Check after the time is up and if not done, and let it AIR FRY for one more minute.
11. Once it is done, serve.

Fried Oreos

Prep time: 2 minutes | Cook time: 8 minutes | Serves 8

- 1 can Pillsbury Crescent Dough (or equivalent)
- 8 Oreo cookies
- 1–2 tablespoons powdered sugar

1. Open the crescent dough up and cut it into the right-size pieces to completely wrap each cookie.
2. Wrap each Oreo in dough. Make sure that there are no air bubbles and that the cookies are completely covered.
3. Install a crisper plate in both drawers. Place half the Oreo cookies in the zone 1 drawer and half in zone 2's. Sprinkle the tops with the powdered sugar, then insert the drawers into the unit.
4. Select zone 1, select AIR FRY, set temperature to 390 degrees F/ 200 degrees C, and set time to 8 minutes. Select MATCH to match zone 2 settings to zone 1. Press the START/STOP button to begin cooking.
5. Serve warm and enjoy!

Grilled Peaches
Prep time: 5 minutes | Cook time: 10 minutes | Serves 4

- 2 yellow peaches
- ¼ cup graham cracker crumbs
- ¼ cup brown sugar
- ¼ cup butter, diced into tiny cubes
- Whipped cream or ice cream, for serving.

1. Cut the peaches into wedges and pull out their pits.
2. Install a crisper plate in both drawers. Put half of the peach wedges into the drawer in zone 1 and half in zone 2's. Sprinkle the tops of the wedges with the crumbs, sugar, and butter. Insert the drawers into the unit.
3. Select zone 1, select AIR FRY, set the temperature to 390 degrees F/ 200 degrees C, and set the time to 10 minutes. Select MATCH to match zone 2 settings to zone 1. Press the START/STOP button to begin cooking.

Strawberry Nutella Hand Pies
Prep time: 20 minutes | Cook time: 10 minutes | Serves 8

- 1 tube pie crust dough
- 3–4 strawberries, finely chopped
- Nutella
- Sugar
- Coconut oil cooking spray

1. Roll out the pie dough and place it on a baking sheet. Cut out hearts using a 3-inch heart-shaped cookie cutter as precisely as possible.
2. Gather the leftover dough into a ball and roll it out thinly to make a few more heart shapes. For 8 hand pies, I was able to get 16 hearts from one tube of pie crust.
3. Set aside a baking tray lined with parchment paper.
4. Spread a dollop of Nutella (approximately 1 teaspoon) on one of the hearts. Add a few strawberry pieces to the mix. Add a pinch of sugar to the top.
5. Place another heart on top and use a fork to tightly crimp the edges. Gently poke holes in the top of the pie with a fork. Place on a baking sheet. Repeat for all the pies.
6. All of the pies on the tray should be sprayed with coconut oil.
7. Install a crisper plate in both drawers. Place half the pies in the zone 1 drawer and half in zone 2's, then insert the drawers into the unit.
8. Select zone 1, select BAKE, set temperature to 390 degrees F/ 200 degrees C, and set time to 10 minutes. Select MATCH to match zone 2 settings to zone 1. Press the START/STOP button to begin cooking.

Baked Apples
Prep time: 5 minutes | Cook time: 20 minutes | Serves 4

- 4 granny smith apples, halved and cored
- ¼ cup old-fashioned oats (not the instant kind)
- 1 tablespoon butter, melted
- 2 tablespoon brown sugar
- ½ teaspoon ground cinnamon
- Whipped cream, for topping (optional)

1. Insert the crisper plates into the drawers. Lay the cored apple halves in a single layer into each of the drawers (the apple's flesh should be pointing up). Insert the drawers into the unit.
2. Select zone 1, select AIR FRY, set temperature to 350 degrees F/ 175 degrees C, and set time to 10 minutes. Select MATCH to match zone 2 settings to zone 1. Press the START/STOP button to begin cooking.
3. Meanwhile, mix the oats, melted butter, brown sugar, and cinnamon to form the topping.
4. Add the topping to the apple halves when they've cooked for 10 minutes.
5. Select zone 1, select BAKE, set temperature to 390 degrees F/ 200 degrees C, and set time to 22 minutes. Select MATCH to match zone 2 settings to zone 1. Press the START/STOP button to begin cooking.
6. Serve warm and enjoy!

Cinnamon Sugar Dessert Fries
Prep time: 5 minutes | Cook time: 15 minutes | Serves 4

- 2 sweet potatoes
- 1 tablespoon butter, melted
- 1 teaspoon butter, melted
- 2 tablespoons sugar
- ½ teaspoon ground cinnamon

1. Peel and cut the sweet potatoes into skinny fries.
2. Coat the fries with 1 tablespoon of butter.
3. Install a crisper plate into each drawer. Place half the sweet potatoes in the zone 1 drawer and half in zone 2's, then insert the drawers into the unit.
4. Select zone 1, select AIR FRY, set temperature to 390 degrees F/ 200 degrees C, and set time to 15 minutes. Select MATCH to match zone 2 settings to zone 1. Press the START/STOP button to begin cooking.
5. When the time reaches 11 minutes, press START/STOP to pause the unit. Remove the drawers and flip the fries. Re-insert the drawers into the unit and press START/STOP to resume cooking.
6. Meanwhile, mix the 1 teaspoon of butter, the sugar, and the cinnamon in a large bowl.
7. When the fries are done, add them to the bowl, and toss them to coat.
8. Serve and enjoy!

Lava Cake

Prep time: 10 minutes | Cook time: 10 minutes | Serves 4

- 1 cup semi-sweet chocolate chips
- 8 tablespoons butter
- 4 eggs
- 2 teaspoons vanilla extract
- ½ teaspoon salt
- 6 tablespoons all-purpose flour
- 1 cup powdered sugar
- 2 tablespoons Nutella
- 1 tablespoon butter, softened
- 1 tablespoon powdered sugar

1. Heat the chocolate chips and butter in a medium-sized microwave-safe bowl in 30-second intervals until thoroughly melted and smooth, stirring after each interval.
2. Whisk together the eggs, vanilla, salt, flour, and powdered sugar in a mixing bowl.
3. Combine the Nutella, softened butter, and powdered sugar in a separate bowl.
4. Spray 4 ramekins with oil and fill them halfway with the chocolate chip mixture. Fill each ramekin halfway with Nutella, then top with the remaining chocolate chip mixture, making sure the Nutella is well covered.
5. Install a crisper plate in both drawers. Place 2 ramekins in each drawer and insert the drawers into the unit.
6. Select zone 1, select AIR FRY, set temperature to 390 degrees F/ 200 degrees C, and set time to 22 minutes. Select MATCH to match zone 2 settings to zone 1. Press the START/STOP button to begin cooking.
7. Serve hot.

Jelly Donuts

Prep time: 5 minutes | Cook time: 5 minutes | Serves 4

- 1 package Pillsbury Grands (Homestyle)
- ½ cup seedless raspberry jelly
- 1 tablespoon butter, melted
- ½ cup sugar

1. Install a crisper plate in both drawers. Place half of the biscuits in the zone 1 drawer and half in zone 2's, then insert the drawers into the unit. You may need to cook in batches.
2. Select zone 1, select AIR FRY, set temperature to 390 degrees F/ 200 degrees C, and set time to 22 minutes. Select MATCH to match zone 2 settings to zone 1. Press the START/STOP button to begin cooking.
3. Place the sugar into a wide bowl with a flat bottom.
4. Baste all sides of the cooked biscuits with the melted butter and roll in the sugar to cover completely.
5. Using a long cake tip, pipe 1–2 tablespoons of raspberry jelly into each biscuit. You've now got raspberry-filled donuts!

Appendix 1 Measurement Conversion Chart

WEIGHT EQUIVALENTS	
US STANDARD	METRIC (APPROXIMATE)
1 ounce	28 g
2 ounces	57 g
5 ounces	142 g
10 ounces	284 g
15 ounces	425 g
16 ounces (1 pound)	455 g
1.5pounds	680 g
2pounds	907 g

TEMPERATURES EQUIVALENTS	
FAHRENHEIT (F)	CELSIUS (C) (APPROXIMATE)
225 °F	107 °C
250 °F	120 °C
275 °F	135 °C
300 °F	150 °C
325 °F	160 °C
350 °F	180 °C
375 °F	190 °C
400 °F	205 °C
425 °F	220 °C
450 °F	235 °C
475 °F	245 °C
500 °F	260 °C

VOLUME EQUIVALENTS (DRY)	
US STANDARD	METRIC (APPROXIMATE)
⅛ teaspoon	0.5 mL
¼ teaspoon	1 mL
½ teaspoon	2 mL
¾ teaspoon	4 mL
1 teaspoon	5 mL
1 tablespoon	15 mL
¼ cup	59 mL
½ cup	118 mL
¾ cup	177 mL
1 cup	235 mL
2 cups	475 mL
3 cups	700 mL
4 cups	1 L

VOLUME EQUIVALENTS (LIQUID)		
US STANDARD	US STANDARD (OUNCES)	US STANDARD (OUNCES)
2 tablespoons	1 fl.oz	30 mL
¼ cup	2 fl.oz	60 mL
½ cup	4 fl.oz	120 mL
1 cup	8 fl.oz	240 mL
1½ cup	12 fl.oz	355 mL
2 cups or 1 pint	16 fl.oz	475 mL
4 cups or 1 quart	32 fl.oz	1 L

Appendix 2 Air Fryer Cooking Chart

Meat and Seafood	Temp	Time (min)
Bacon	400°F	5 to 10
Beef Eye Round Roast (4 lbs.)	390°F	45 to 55
Bone to in Pork Chops	400°F	4 to 5 per side
Brats	400°F	8 to 10
Burgers	350°F	8 to 10
Chicken Breast	375°F	22 to 23
Chicken Tender	400°F	14 to 16
Chicken Thigh	400°F	25
Chicken Wings (2 lbs.)	400°F	10 to 12
Cod	370°F	8 to 10
Fillet Mignon (8 oz.)	400°F	14 to 18
Fish Fillet (0.5 lb., 1-inch)	400°F	10
Flank Steak (1.5 lbs.)	400°F	10 to 14
Lobster Tails (4 oz.)	380°F	5 to 7
Meatballs	400°F	7 to 10
Meat Loaf	325°F	35 to 45
Pork Chops	375°F	12 to 15
Salmon	400°F	5 to 7
Salmon Fillet (6 oz.)	380°F	12
Sausage Patties	400°F	8 to 10
Shrimp	375°F	8
Steak	400°F	7 to 14
Tilapia	400°F	8 to 12
Turkey Breast (3 lbs.)	360°F	40 to 50
Whole Chicken (6.5 lbs.)	360°F	75

Desserts	Temp	Time (min)
Apple Pie	320°F	30
Brownies	350°F	17
Churros	360°F	13
Cookies	350°F	5
Cupcakes	330°F	11
Doughnuts	360°F	5
Roasted Bananas	375°F	8
Peaches	350°F	5

Frozen Foods	Temp	Time (min)
Breaded Shrimp	400°F	9
Chicken Burger	360°F	11
Chicken Nudgets	400°F	10
Corn Dogs	400°F	7
Curly Fries (1 to 2 lbs.)	400°F	11 to 14
Fish Sticks (10 oz.)	400°F	10
French Fries	380°F	15 to 20
Hash Brown	360°F	15 to 18
Meatballs	380°F	6 to 8
Mozzarella Sticks	400°F	8
Onion Rings (8 oz.)	400°F	8
Pizza	390°F	5 to 10
Pot Pie	360°F	25
Pot Sticks (10 oz.)	400°F	8
Sausage Rolls	400°F	15
Spring Rolls	400°F	15 to 20

Vegetables	Temp	Time (min)
Asparagus	375°F	4 to 6
Baked Potatoes	400°F	35 to 45
Broccoli	400°F	8 to 10
Brussels Sprouts	350°F	15 to 18
Butternut Squash (cubed)	375°F	20 to 25
Carrots	375°F	15 to 25
Cauliflower	400°F	10 to 12
Corn on the Cob	390°F	6
Eggplant	400°F	15
Green Beans	375°F	16 to 20
Kale	250°F	12
Mushrooms	400°F	5
Peppers	375°F	8 to 10
Sweet Potatoes (whole)	380°F	30 to 35
Tomatoes (halved, sliced)	350°F	10
Zucchini (½-inch sticks)	400°F	12

Appendix 3 Index

A

all-purpose flour 50, 53
allspice 15
almond 5, 14
ancho chile 10
ancho chile powder 5
apple 9
apple cider vinegar 9
arugula 51
avocado 11

B

bacon 52
balsamic vinegar 7, 12, 52
basil 5, 8, 11, 13
beet 52
bell pepper 50, 51, 53
black beans 50, 51
broccoli 51, 52, 53
buns 52
butter 50

C

canola oil 50, 51, 52
carrot 52, 53
cauliflower 5, 52
cayenne 5, 52
cayenne pepper 52
Cheddar cheese 52
chicken 6
chili powder 50, 51
chipanle pepper 50
chives 5, 6, 52
cinnamon 15
coconut 6
Colby Jack cheese 51
coriander 52
corn 50, 51
corn kernels 50
cumin 5, 10, 15, 50, 51, 52

D

diced panatoes 50
Dijon mustard 7, 12, 13, 51
dry onion powder 52

E

egg 14, 50, 53
enchilada sauce 51

F

fennel seed 53
flour 50, 53
fresh chives 5, 6, 52
fresh cilantro 52
fresh cilantro leaves 52
fresh dill 5
fresh parsley 6, 52
fresh parsley leaves 52

G

garlic 5, 9, 10, 11, 13, 14, 50, 51, 52, 53
garlic powder 8, 9, 52, 53

H

half-and-half 50
hemp seeds 8
honey 9, 51

I

instant rice 51

K

kale 14
kale leaves 14
ketchup 53
kosher salt 5, 10, 15

L

lemon 5, 6, 14, 51, 53
lemon juice 6, 8, 11, 13, 14, 51
lime 9, 12
lime juice 9, 12
lime zest 9, 12

M

maple syrup 7, 12, 53
Marinara Sauce 5
micro greens 52
milk 5, 50
mixed berries 12
Mozzarella 50, 53
Mozzarella cheese 50, 53
mushroom 51, 52
mustard 51, 53
mustard powder 53

N

nutritional yeast 5

O

olive oil 5, 12, 13, 14, 50, 51, 52, 53
onion 5, 50, 51
onion powder 8
oregano 5, 8, 10, 50

P

panatoes 50, 52
paprika 5, 15, 52
Parmesan cheese 51, 53
parsley 6, 52
pesto 52
pink Himalayan salt 5, 7, 8, 11
pizza dough 50, 53
pizza sauce 50
plain coconut yogurt 6
plain Greek yogurt 5
porcini powder 53
potato 53

R

Ranch dressing 52
raw honey 9, 12, 13
red pepper flakes 5, 8, 14, 15, 51, 53
ricotta cheese 53

S

saffron 52
Serrano pepper 53
sugar 10
summer squash 51

T

tahini 5, 8, 9, 11
thyme 50
toasted almonds 14
tomato 5, 50, 52, 53
turmeric 15

U

unsalted butter 50
unsweetened almond milk 5

V

vegetable broth 50
vegetable stock 51

W

white wine 8, 11
wine vinegar 8, 10, 11

Y

yogurt 5, 6

Z

zucchini 50, 51, 52, 53

KAREN A. BURKS

Made in the USA
Coppell, TX
19 September 2023

21735791R00044